Finding the Concept, Not Just the Word

CHANDOS
INFORMATION PROFESSIONAL SERIES

Series Editor: Ruth Rikowski
(email: Rikowskigr@aol.com)

Chandos' new series of books are aimed at the busy information professional. They have been specially commissioned to provide the reader with an authoritative view of current thinking. They are designed to provide easy-to-read and (most importantly) practical coverage of topics that are of interest to librarians and other information professionals. If you would like a full listing of current and forthcoming titles, please visit our website **www.chandospublishing.com** or contact Hannah Grace-Williams on email info@chandospublishing.com or telephone number +44 (0) 1993 848726.

New authors: we are always pleased to receive ideas for new titles; if you would like to write a book for Chandos, please contact Dr Glyn Jones on email gjones@chandospublishing.com or telephone number +44 (0) 1993 848726.

Bulk orders: some organisations buy a number of copies of our books. If you are interested in doing this, we would be pleased to discuss a discount. Please contact Hannah Grace-Williams on email info@chandospublishing.com or telephone number +44 (0) 1993 848726.

Finding the Concept, Not Just the Word: A librarian's guide to ontologies and semantics

Brandy E. King
and
Kathy Reinold

Chandos Publishing
Oxford · England

Chandos Publishing (Oxford) Limited
TBAC Business Centre
Avenue 4
Station Lane
Witney
Oxford OX28 4BN
UK
Tel: +44 (0) 1993 848726 Fax: +44 (0) 1865 884448
Email: info@chandospublishing.com
www.chandospublishing.com

First published in Great Britain in 2008

ISBN:
978 1 84334 318 9 (paperback)
978 1 84334 319 6 (hardback)
1 84334 318 5 (paperback)
1 84334 319 3 (hardback)

British Library Cataloguing-in-Publication Data.
A catalogue record for this book is available from the British Library.

Typeset by Domex e-Data Pvt. Ltd.

Contents

About the authors

Brandy King is the Information Specialist at the Center on Media and Child Health at Children's Hospital Boston. She is a graduate of Smith College (BA) and Simmons College (MLIS). She is an active member of the Special Libraries Association and was the recipient of the 2005 SLA Innovation in Technology Award for the creation of a customized media effects ontology used for semantic searching.

Kathy Reinold is a software consultant for Tessella, Inc. She is a graduate of Emmanuel College (BA Mathematics) and Boston University (MS Computer Science). She is also a Springboard Enterprises alumna, a member of Women Entrepreneurs in Science and Technology, and a member of the Association of Computing Machinery. Ms. Reinold has extensive experience in software development and methodologies including work on ontologies and semantic search.

The authors may be contacted via the publishers.

Preface

In June 2003 I accepted an assignment as the librarian for the Center on Media and Child Health (CMCH). My task was to create a database of all existing research on the connections between the health of children and adolescents, and the influence of media such as TV, video games, and the internet. This project was expected to take three months; five years later, I am still at it. This is a testament to the enormity of the research collection I found, to advancements in web technology and knowledge management, and to the variety of ways I can use my skills as an information professional to contribute to the goals of CMCH.

In 2004, at a knowledge management meeting, I saw a demonstration of a semantic search technology showing how a user could ask a question in natural language and receive results that got at the meaning behind the question, rather than just matching the keywords as most search engines do. I was impressed. Since I had been pondering for weeks the challenge of serving a varied audience made up of parents, teachers, and multidisciplinary researchers, I was intrigued by the possibilities this technology presented for the CMCH Database of Research.

Apparently not all business deals are 'made on the golf course', since one of the most important encounters of the day (resulting in a solution to my challenge and eventually in this book) took place in the ladies' room as I left the meeting. The search tool I had seen was from SemanTx Life Sciences, Inc., and while I was on my way out, Kathy Reinold and

I discussed the great opportunity for SemanTx Life Sciences technology to improve CMCH website users' access to information about media and health. That was the beginning of a partnership in which SemanTx Life Sciences contributed staff time, expertise, and technology to create a natural language search engine for the CMCH Database of Research. Along the way, Kathy took the time to explain the technology to me, to help outline a structure for the CMCH ontology, and to make improvements once the search engine was established.

As I came to realize the power of ontologies and semantics, I began to tell other librarians about them, showing my work as a case study of how they could be applied. In 2005 I received the Innovations in Technology Award from the Special Libraries Association (SLA), and in 2005 and 2006 I wrote papers describing the construction of the database and comparing the precision and recall of Boolean versus semantic searches. This led to an invitation to author this book about ontologies and semantic search, geared toward providing practical information for librarians.

I would like to thank my colleagues, whose skills and support have made the partnership between SemanTx Life Sciences, Inc., and CMCH possible: Sharon Gray, MLIS, whose encouragement and suave networking skills enabled me to move forward with the CMCH/SemanTx Life Sciences partnership; Michael Rich, MD MPH, and the staff of CMCH, who have championed collaboration and innovative thinking about media and child health, especially Scott Stoneburner, MLIS, who outlined the majority of the structure for the CMCH ontology; Dr. Ken Baclawski of Northeastern University, who provided the original research and patents that led to the SemanTx Life Sciences technology; and Michael Belanger and the staff of SemanTx Life Sciences, who provide ongoing support for SmartSearch on the CMCH website.

Kathy and I would like to thank those whose contributions to this book are significant and whose experience and observations grounded this work in reality:

- Tonya Hongsermeier, MD MBA, Corporate Manager of Clinical Knowledge Management and Decision Support, and her colleague Vipul Kashyap, PhD, Senior Medical Informatician, who both enthusiastically described the work being done at Partners HealthCare.
- Aaron Mannes, Terrorism Researcher and Project Director, who provided insight on how the Maryland Information and Network Dynamics Lab Semantic Web Agents Project (MINDSWAP) created and maintains the Profiles in Terror ontology.
- William Hayes, PhD, Ekaterina Mantrova, MD PhD, and Phoebe Roberts, PhD, from Biogen Idec, who explained their work with thesauri within library and information services.
- Ken Baclawski, PhD, of Northeastern University, who has been involved in the semantic web since its inception and graciously spent time reviewing our chapters for technical accuracy.

Kathy thanks her husband, Bob Miller, and daughter, Danielle DeNufrio, for support, understanding, and editing. Her gratitude is also extended to a core of extraordinary family, friends, and mentors for encouragement and support over the years.

I thank my family and friends, most notably Rachel Herzig-Marx, who spent every Saturday for six months watching me work on this book. To my family – Amberly, Jeff, and Ilda King – and my husband Stephen Palumbo: thank you for your constant support of and belief in my professional ambitions; this book would not have been possible without your encouragement.

Kathy and I hope that this book will provide an understandable view of ontologies and semantics, showcase their power to transform how information is organized and found, and inspire librarians to partner as leaders with computer programmers, knowledge managers, and subject experts as the semantic web becomes a reality.

Brandy King, MLIS

Introduction

Librarians are often seen as detectives who are trained to know where and how to look for answers. And although that perception is right, we are also constantly performing the role of a translator, interpreting information every step of the way from listening to a patron's question to presenting them with an answer. We provide context for the question, filling in details that ultimately enable us to fulfill the detective role. These critical details allow us to pinpoint which databases or search engines to use, to determine what constitutes high-quality information for this particular need, and to create a document or statement that contains the answer the patron is looking for.

Translation occurs at each of the three phases of the librarian–patron interaction: the reference interview, the search itself, and the formulation of an answer.

Conducting a reference interview

When conducting a reference interview, we consider our past experiences with search engines and with patrons themselves to help formulate context for the question. We connect what a patron asks for with what else is out there – other topics connected to it, how old the information might be, and where we might look for an answer.

We might consider context such as:

- *Existing answer* – Does the patron know for sure that this information exists? Has she seen a newspaper article on the topic but can't remember where? Or is she looking for a dissertation topic, thus hoping that it has *not* been researched before?

- *Date range* – From what time period will the answer be appropriate? Is the patron looking for medical information, in which case, is the most current information necessary? Or is she hoping to find out more about an original document, which is often cited?
- *Patron experience and education* – What experience does the patron already have? If the patron is looking for information on flowers, is she a florist with a high level of knowledge? Or is she a new homeowner wanting to spruce up her small garden plot?
- *Answer form* – What will the patron do with the information once she has it? Is she wanting to satisfy her own curiosity? Or is she intending to make a presentation on the topic?

Executing the search

After gathering the information in the reference interview, librarians translate it into a search strategy, consciously or unconsciously. We check off in our heads which sources we think may contain the information we are looking for. Often, determining where to look first leads to decisions on how that search will be constructed (Table 0.1).

Regardless of the strategy selected for the task, in today's search environment we are ultimately relying on text matching. We are seeking for a word we enter into a search engine to match a word in a record. We are translating the essence of the patron's question into words we *think* the record *might* contain.

Table 0.1 **Search strategies used for different sources**

Source	Search strategy
Internet search engine	String together keywords, enclose phrases in quotes
Internet directory	Browse through hierarchical lists of categories
Academic database	Enter keywords, choose from a list of subject headings, use Boolean logic, narrow search parameters by pre-defined fields such as age range, study design, publication type

For example, if the patron is looking for reviews of newly released video games, we turn to a search engine and enter text that might match with the idea of video games. We might just try a quick search for the phrase 'video games' and examine the results. If the patron is a ten-year-old boy looking for new and fun games to play, this list of results may be enough. But what if the patron is an executive in the video game industry who wants to know which games are getting good reviews so that she can incorporate aspects of those games into her own? She will need a more comprehensive list, one where the librarian searches using all possible ways of expressing the patron's information need. At the heart of the question is the concept of an interactive game that is played electronically with a graphic display. The phrase 'video games' is just one name for that concept. They are also called computer games, electronic games, and virtual reality. In order to make a comprehensive search, the librarian can either carry out a Boolean search using all these terms strung together by 'OR', or she could try to match the concept 'video games' with a subject heading chosen to represent all the different names for that one concept.

Simply put, when the text entered in a search box matches the text in a record, the record is returned as a search result.

Although a text search may bring up hundreds (or even thousands) of records, two problems are typically encountered:

- We are missing records that match the conceptual content of our search because the exact text was not matched. For example, if we search for *brooches* but do not receive results where the items are called *pins* rather than *brooches*.
- We are retrieving records where the text matches, but the context of the article may show that the words are not conceptually related to our needs, for example, when looking for computers, we type in *apple* and receive recipes, apple-picking locations, and information on how to grow an apple tree in addition to information on the company Apple Inc.

In the first problem, we miss out on records that may be just as relevant as, or in some cases more relevant than, the records in our result list. To turn back to our video games example, according to the ranking feature on the Thumbshots website (*http://ranking.thumbshots.com/*), if a Google search for *video games* produces 100 results and a Google search for *computer games* produces 100 results, only 13 of those results are the same. This means that in either of the searches, users are missing 87 other results that are relevant because the search engine only looks for matching *text*, not matching *concepts*.

In the second problem, we waste time filtering through results that are irrelevant to our needs. We would be finding articles that mention video games once, as a passing thought, in the larger context of adolescent leisure time. We could even find an article titled 'This Article is NOT About Video Games' simply because the text phrase 'video games' is present both in the query and in the record.

At its most basic level, text matching searches lack context. If a whole article focuses on one concept, but does not use the word you chose to enter as a query, you will miss that result entirely.

Presenting the answer

Once the librarian receives a list of search results, she evaluates each result to see if the source is reliable and if it answers the question entirely, re-searching for more authoritative sources or more complete results if necessary. When the librarian has a list of sources that satisfy the patron's information need, she translates what she found into a form the patron can best use for her purpose.

But what if... ?

What if instead of translating the patron's question into a search strategy, the librarian asked a question and the search engine did the work of translation? What if the search engine could 'read' the question, search a list of synonyms, and explore conceptually related topics? For example, searching for video games could return results for video games, computer games, electronic games, virtual reality, and more. Would it present a more well-rounded search? Would it save time for the librarian?

In short, **what if the search engine understood the concepts in the question, rather than just matching the text?**

This is all possible with the use of ontologies and semantic technologies. This book will take librarians from theory to practice, providing a plain-language explanation of semantic technologies, a behind-the-scenes understanding of how ontologies are constructed, and case studies that demonstrate how these tools are being applied in the real world to make the discovery of information more robust.

Part 1 of this book gives a general overview of ontologies and the semantic web. In Chapter 1, readers will learn about the history of ontologies and discover their similarities to and differences from other knowledge structures such as dictionaries, thesauri, and taxonomies. Chapter 2 provides an overview of semantic search engines, enabling the reader to understand how these engines connect to and draw from ontologies to comprehend the essence of a user's query.

We describe how to construct an ontology from the ground up, gathering terms, arranging them into categories, and adding relationships in Chapter 3. And in Chapter 4 we construct an ontology by customizing and adding onto an existing knowledge structure.

Part 2 describes in a more detailed fashion how semantic technologies work. Chapter 5 explains how natural language processing is applied so that computers can extract meaning from text; Chapter 6 focuses on how to associate semantic information with documents; Chapter 7 shows a variety of other semantic capabilities including classification, topic maps, and rules engines.

Readers should now have an understanding of where ontologies and semantic search engines originated from, how they are constructed, and how they perform. Part 3 presents four case studies in which semantic technologies are solving problems in different industries.

Chapter 8 describes how Biogen Idec is using text-mining techniques to shorten the lengthy research process in drug discovery. Chapter 9 explores how the Center on Media and Child Health is providing a natural language search mechanism so that parents can examine evidence-based information from which they can make decisions about their family's media use.

Chapter 10 describes how Partners HealthCare is applying semantics to arm clinical staff with best practice guidelines and the most up-to-date information for treating patients. Chapter 11 examines how MINDSWAP is using ontologies to aid intelligence analysts in describing relationships between terrorists.

In Part 4, readers are presented with advanced topics such as detailed explanations about languages for expressing ontologies and tools for building ontologies. Chapter 14 in Part 5 provides insight into the challenges and opportunities that the semantic web presents and offers recommendations for those who want to join in the movement toward the next version of the web.

Ontologies and semantics have the power to transform the future of knowledge management for librarians and the public. Ontologies provide a powerful framework in which to make connections between ideas, literature, and disciplines, resulting in opportunities to deliver conceptual bodies of knowledge to people whose curiosity or business needs lead them to ask questions. By contributing to the creation of ontologies used to aid in semantic search, librarians can make the transition from their role as translators between the public and search engines to one where they contribute to the translation taking place *inside* the search engine, empowering users to ask their own questions in their own words.

Part 1
Understanding ontologies

Our brains do not just store words, they store meaning; they make semantic connections. They connect words with other words, with previously stored information, with sounds, smells, places. Can computers be made to understand these connections?

Ontologies are at the heart of semantics. Their structure allows not only for hierarchical and synonymous relationships as seen in other knowledge structures, but also for any number of meaningful connections such as diagnosed_by, result_of, cooked_with, powered_by, married_to, and a host of others. By allowing words to be connected to other words in this fashion, a well-rounded picture of an entire concept can be developed and a computer can understand meaning.

Part 1 of this book will show how our brains organize information, how computers understand information, and how ontologies are constructed.

1

Organizing knowledge

Humans have always had a need to organize information. We name things, organize them into groups, determine how the groups are related, and make generalizations about behavior and capability based on our groupings. For example, Royal Canadian Mounted Police officers, Massachusetts State Troopers, FBI agents, and a small town sheriff are all related in our minds because we consider them each a part of the greater law enforcement community. Organization helps us understand and retain information better and also helps us to locate information when we need it.

The human brain is the quintessential information organizer; the brain makes connections between old and new information to build a network of inter-related ideas or events. It is relating and organizing constantly. Some connections become obvious when we are given context. For example, if we are in a doctor's office speaking to a physician who recommends a spinal tap, we recognize that she is not referring to the musical group, but to a medical procedure.

Other connections in our brains may be less obvious. We have all encountered a sensory experience triggering a memory. A whiff of gasoline takes you back to your first road trip when you were 16. Hearing a song on the radio instantly reminds you of an 8th grade dance. Although we may not be conscious of the connection, our brains store relationships between things like sensory experiences, objects, events, and ideas. Whether obvious or subtle, these represent meaningful links; they are *semantic* links.

Librarians are masters of organizing information. They have defined techniques for organizing information including identifying keywords, subject headings, taxonomies, and classification systems. These are all associative methods that follow the model of how our brains work. Librarians can impose order on the knowledge provided by material from typical print resources such as books, magazines, and websites to other formats such as audio, film, maps, and photographs. The general public relies on librarians to impose order on these items so that information can be found quickly and consistently no matter where it is located.

The Dewey Decimal System, devised in the 1870s, is the most widely used classification system in the world (OCLC, 2007). A person looking for books on religion would be able to find them labeled 200 whether they were in a library in Egypt or the US. This consistency of classification is essential to fulfilling specific information needs quickly among an overwhelming sea of knowledge.

Over the past few decades, the prevalence of personal computers, the internet and the World Wide Web have exponentially increased the amount of electronic data accessible to the average person. A major challenge librarians face today is that the millions of pages of knowledge maintained electronically are not organized by a universal classification system.

Yahoo! has attempted to create a directory for the web by arranging websites into categories. Their top level of categories includes grouping such as Arts & Humanities, Education, Health, and Science. Yet because thousands of pages are added, deleted, and updated daily it is virtually impossible to know whether all pages have been categorized at any one time.

Though Google also has a directory, the company is most well known for its search engine. Having a search engine minimizes the need for a universal system of web organization since the search engine finds information based on text matches. If a user enters a search for *martial arts*, the search engine looks for pages containing that exact text. The limitation of this kind of engine is that it does not look for related terms such as *karate* or *jiu jitsu*. But Google has allowed for flexibility within text matching by offering the capability of nearly exact text matches. If a user misspells her query and enters a search for *marital arts*, it will reply with the question: *Did you mean martial arts?*

Google and Yahoo! are two of the most well-known search engines in the world, yet they do not organize information by employing the associations our brain makes so easily. Is there technology available that exploits those connections to tame the volume of information available?

From the first attempt at automated computation by Alan Turing in 1931, computers have been modeled after the human brain. Alan Turing actually described developing a computing machine as 'building a brain'. He aspired to enable his universal machine 'to acquire and exhibit the faculties of the human mind' (Hodges, 2007). John von Neumann, another early pioneer in computer technology, viewed computers not merely as number-crunching machines, but as problem-solving machines. His unfinished work *The Computer and the Brain*, published in 1958, draws parallels between the human brain and the computer (von Neumann, 1958).

Hyperlinks represent another attempt to make computers 'exhibit the faculties of the human mind' (von Neumann, 1958). In 1965 Ted Nelson first defined the term hypertext; he envisioned hypertext to be non-sequential text that readers could explore in many ways, providing 'alternate pathways for people who think different ways' (Nelson, 1978). Hyperlinks provide a partial implementation of this vision and are now commonplace in our use of the internet. Links on web pages are designed to mimic the brain's connections. The author of the page links a word or phrase to another page where the reader can find more information on that topic. The connection between the two pages may not be immediately clear to the reader, but because it exists in the mind of the author it is a meaningful relationship, a *semantic* link.

Although he is the first to admit that a series of observations and accomplishments by many distinguished people paved the way, Tim Berners-Lee is generally credited with the invention of the World Wide Web. He extended the concepts of hypertext and computer networks to imagine a network of knowledge connected by hyperlinks. Influenced by his mathematician parents, Berners-Lee was thinking about how to make computers intuitive as early as in his high school years. At CERN (the European organization for nuclear research) he had access to the largest internet node in Europe. He first brought together Ted Nelson's notion of hypertext and the internet to 'invent' the World Wide Web. In his book *Weaving the Web* (Berners-Lee, 1999), Berners-Lee describes his two-part dream for the web. The first role for the web is as a powerful tool for collaboration. Although the web today certainly allows for collaboration, it is mostly known as a worldwide communication channel and marketplace. The second part of his dream is for the web to be a place where machines can analyze data and understand the content supplied by humans. If machines could make the semantic connections that our brains do, they could 'understand'. Berners-Lee and others are still working on this second part today, as currently our search engines allow us to search for words within documents, but they do not allow us to search for ideas.

Essentially, Berners-Lee's vision asks: What if the information available on the web was organized based on its semantic content, on its meaning? What if users could try to fill their information needs by asking a question in their language – natural English – of a search engine? What if a classification system was based on semantic connections between subjects, and users could discover new relationships by exploring connections? How can we create the semantic connections that would enable such a powerful web of information? The answer is by creating ontologies.

What is an ontology?

The term ontology has its roots in philosophy; it is defined as the study of being or the nature of existence. The concept of ontology dates back to Aristotle, who defined ten basic categories into which all entities, ideas, and objects in the universe could be classified. Although the term ontology is clearly defined for the discipline of philosophy, a number of definitions have been formulated for the definition as it relates to knowledge management and information technology. In 1993 Tom Gruber, who pioneered the use of the web for knowledge sharing, defined an ontology as 'a description (like a formal specification of a program) of the concepts and relationships that can exist for an agent or a community of agents' (Gruber, 1993).

This is the World Wide Web Consortium's (W3C's) definition of an ontology:

> An ontology defines the terms used to describe and represent an area of knowledge. The semantic web

> needs ontologies with a significant degree of structure. These need to specify descriptions for the following kinds of concepts:
>
> - Classes (general things) in the many domains of interest.
> - The relationships that can exist among things.
> - The properties (or attributes) those things may have.
>
> Ontologies are usually expressed ... so that detailed, accurate, consistent, sound, and meaningful distinctions can be made among the classes, properties, and relations. (World Wide Web Consortium, 2004b)

There are other definitions, but they all share a few simple characteristics: well-defined concepts, relationships, and a taxonomy. For our purposes in this book, we will define an ontology as *a collection of concepts, arranged in a hierarchy of categories, combined with the relationships between those concepts, in order to reflect the vocabulary of an area of knowledge.*

How are ontologies different from other knowledge representations?

How is an ontology different from a dictionary, a subject heading list or a taxonomy? And what do these differences allow us to do that we could not do previously? Let us first look at common structures and assess how they can be used to organize electronic information, following an example through each description.

The main purpose of a *dictionary* is to define concepts (Figure 1.1).

Figure 1.1 **A dictionary defines concepts**

The format of a dictionary can support more than one definition for each term. Some dictionaries also offer synonyms and other relationships such as antonyms and cross references. Although dictionaries are readily available online and thus able to store electronic information, the arrangement of terms alphabetically does not offer any guidance toward an organization or classification of terms. For example, a dictionary would say that the definition of the concept *car* is 'a motor vehicle with four wheels; usually propelled by an internal combustion engine' (WordNet 3.0, 2008).

The goal of a desk-reference thesaurus like *Roget's* is to list words and their synonymous concepts (Figure 1.2); one concept is equal or similar to another concept, which is equal to a third, fourth, and fifth concept.

To continue our example, a desk-reference thesaurus would say that the concept *car* is equal or similar to the concept *vehicle*, which is equal or similar to the concept *automobile*.

A thesaurus used for cataloging in library science may list more relationships than a desk-reference thesaurus, such as

Figure 1.2 **A thesaurus lists words and their synonymous concepts**

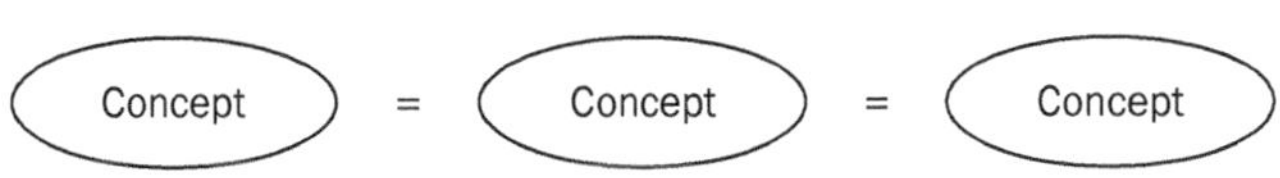

antonyms, cross references, derivatives, variants, and narrower and broader terms. The limitations of both a desk-reference and cataloging thesaurus are that definitions are not provided and relationships between terms are constrained for the most part to *same as*, *opposite of*, *broader than*, and *narrower than*.

The main purpose of a *taxonomy* is to place concepts into a hierarchy where, ideally, each concept appears in one category only (Figure 1.3). The structure is defined in such a way that one concept encompasses another concept, which encompasses another concept, establishing a grouping of broader and narrower concepts.

To continue our example, the concept *transportation* encompasses the concept of *car*, which encompasses the concept of *Ford Mustang*, a specific kind of car. The limitation of taxonomies is that, in the real world, there are many concepts which could belong to more than one category. And although taxonomies offer types of classification, they do not offer definitions and their relationships consist only of *broader than* and *narrower than*.

Neither dictionaries, thesauri, nor taxonomies offer definitions, relationships, and classification all at the same time. Ontologies combine elements of all three of these

Figure 1.3 A taxonomy places concepts into a hierarchy

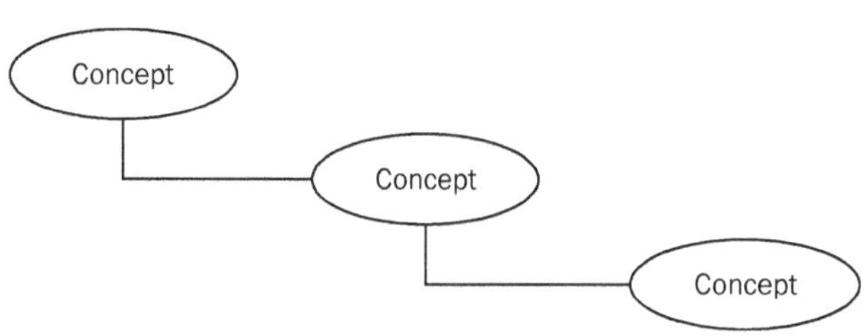

knowledge structures, defining concepts like a dictionary, establishing relationships like a thesaurus, and providing categorization for concepts like a taxonomy. Because each concept is able to be explored from all of these angles, an ontology allows for the exploitation of all the kinds of relationships our brains make automatically (Figure 1.4).

In addition to combining these aspects, an ontology also allows the creator to define an unlimited number of relationships (more precisely than those in a thesaurus), concepts to be represented by phrases instead of just words, and concepts to connect by many different kinds of relationships all at once. These aspects of an ontology allow us to create a web of connections, as depicted in Figure 1.4.

To continue our example, in an ontology the concept *car* would be defined, made equal to the terms *vehicle* and *automobile*, arranged in a taxonomy along with the broader term *transportation* and the narrower term *Ford Mustang*, and then be connected to related terms such as *truck*, *gasoline*, and *steering wheel*, and their definitions.

Figure 1.4 **An ontology allows concepts to be connected through a variety of relationships**

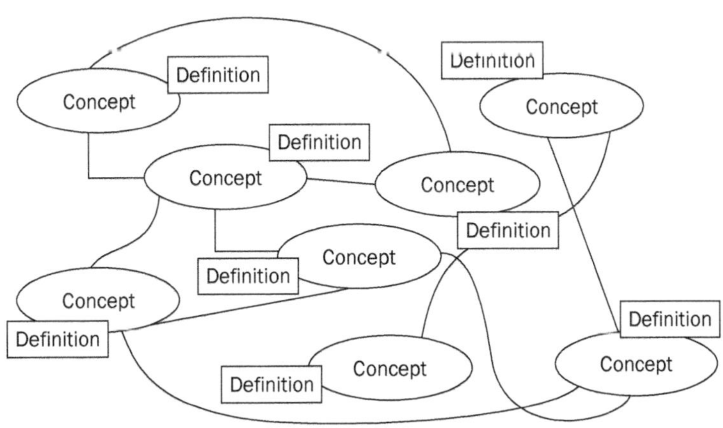

Ontologies are custom-built for each domain to capture its vocabulary along with its unique, expert perspective on the information. The ontology can recognize many ways of identifying the same idea. For example, an ontology can be told to understand that 'filling up' means the same thing as 'getting gas', and that when buying a car you may want to consider 'limited power-train' and 'bumper to bumper' warranties. Just as our brains connect ideas, thoughts, and events into a meaningful web of concepts, so can we build ontologies to perform the same task.

How are ontologies currently being used?

Once this web of ideas and connections is established, how can it be useful to librarians?

Ontologies are being used to:

- standardize vocabulary by publishing concepts, relationships and definitions provided by subject matter experts
- provide better routes of exploration by organizing the information in a more precise and complex way
- provide better search results by using ontology-based search techniques and natural language processing.

Key concepts

- A *semantic link* is a meaningful connection between ideas; the human brain builds a network of inter-related ideas – a network connected by *semantic links*.

- The internet and the World Wide Web have exponentially increased the amount of data available; a system to process vast quantities of electronic data and organize it in meaningful ways is needed.
- The World Wide Web provides 'links' to other documents, but the meanings of the links are not well defined. The *semantic web* will enable semantic links that will carry meaning with them.
- Knowledge structures form the basis for information organization. Table 1.1 compares the characteristics of common knowledge structures; here is an explanation of the terminology:
  - *Organization* may be:
    - alphabetical, which allows one to find known ideas easily
    - relational, which allows one to follow links to related ideas
    - hierarchical, which allows one to follow concepts to more narrowly defined categories.
  - *Synonyms* can be provided to define multiple ways to express an idea.
  - *Definitions* are required to help control how synonyms, categories, or relationships are used.
  - Some structures provide only predefined *relationships* such as antonym, synonym, etc. Others support the creation of other meaningful relationships.
- An *ontology* is a hierarchical collection of concepts and the relationships among those concepts. It typically reflects the vocabulary of domain.
- Current uses of ontologies include standardizing vocabulary, providing better routes of topic exploration, and allowing for search techniques based on natural language parsing.

Table 1.1 **The characteristics of common knowledge structures**

Structure	Purpose	Organization	Synonyms	Definitions	Relationships
Dictionary	Define words	Alphabetical	Sometimes	Yes	Possibly synonym, antonym
Desk-reference thesaurus	Identify synonymous terms	Alphabetical, relational	Yes	No	Limited: antonyms, cross references, derivatives, variants, narrower, broader
Thesaurus for classification system	Organize	Hierarchical	Yes	Sometimes	Limited: narrower, broader
Taxonomy	Organize	Hierarchical	No	No	Limited: narrower, broader
Ontology	Organize, understand	Hierarchical, relational	Yes	Yes, for concepts and relationships	Unlimited, defined by the ontology

2

Ontologies in semantic search

When was the last time that you used your favorite search engine – for example Google, or Yahoo! – and received fewer than 10,000 relevant responses in a search? There is no doubt that the web has much to offer. How do you get to what you really want, without all the extraneous information getting in the way?

Determining whether a search was successful

In determining whether your search was successful, you are likely to ask yourself the following three questions:

- How easy was it to put my information need into a query the search engine could understand?
- Which of the results I received are most relevant to my information need?
- How do I know whether the search engine missed anything important?

Let us look at each of these questions in turn.

How easy was it to express your information need?

In other words, were you able to look for an answer in a way that was straightforward and specific? Most search engines provide a simple interface, consisting of a box on the screen where you type in your query. Although this interface is easy to work with, it may not retrieve the information that you really need because you are typing in a list of words, rather than complete ideas. Let us say that you are trying to answer a specific question. What tools can you use to ask a question directly, instead of translating the question into a string of words? Ask.com (formerly AskJeeves) has tried to position itself in the search engine market as a simple question and answer tool. You may ask 'What semantic search engines are currently available?' (Figure 2.1).

In Figure 2.1, using Ask.com, the first, third, and fifth non-sponsored links discuss the semantic web, not semantic search specifically; the second talks about search trends, which is a relevant topic, but does not locate specific search engines for you. While a majority of casual internet searchers would give up after this search, librarians are usually willing to try a number of different strategies before declaring there is no answer to a question. Looking at the results, you observe that the word 'currently' is not making the search more specific; you drop this word and try a different search tool, Google, where you ask 'What semantic search engines are available?'

In Figure 2.2, using Google, the second entry mentions the phrase *semantic-based* and this sparks an idea: perhaps you should include variants of the word semantic, such as semantically and semantics. Also, if you're looking for products that are available, you could add the word 'sell' to the search query. Now, feeling determined, you decide to try an advanced search using Boolean logic and a different tool:

Figure 2.1 Ask.com results for seacrch 'What semantic search engines are currently available?'

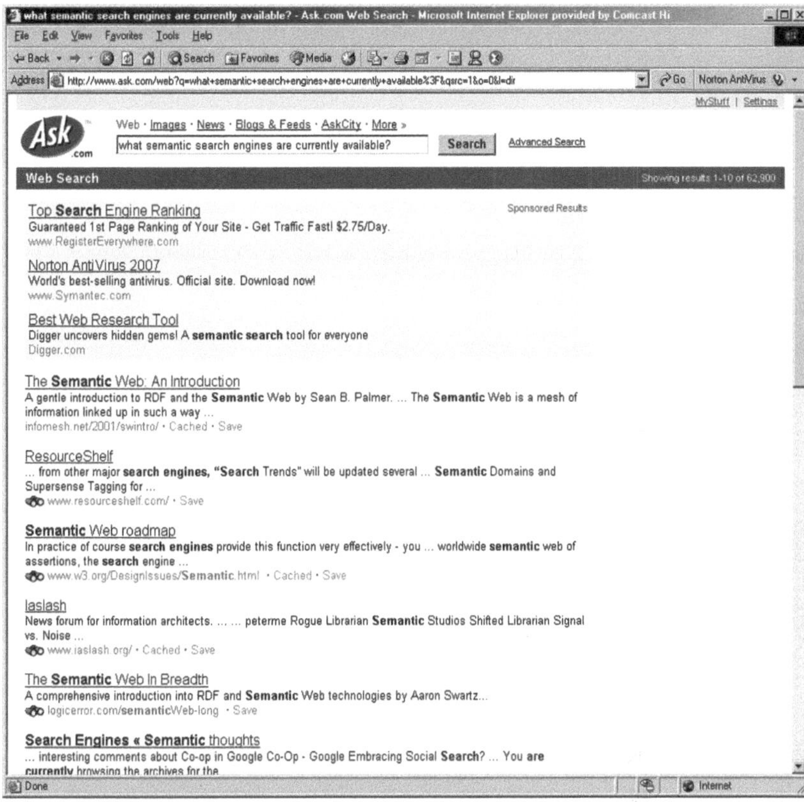

Source: *http://www.ask.com*

Yahoo!. But entering the query sell *(semantic OR semantically OR semantics) AND 'search engine'* still does not retrieve what you were looking for (Figure 2.3).

At this point, a librarian may give up on using a search engine to find an answer, instead turning to a list-serv and asking if other members have ideas, or seeking an expert on semantic search to ask for help.

This example depicts a scene that is repeated many times over in research centers, libraries, offices, and homes every day. Users today, both novice and expert, are familiar with how

Figure 2.2 Google.com results for search 'What semantic search engines are available?'

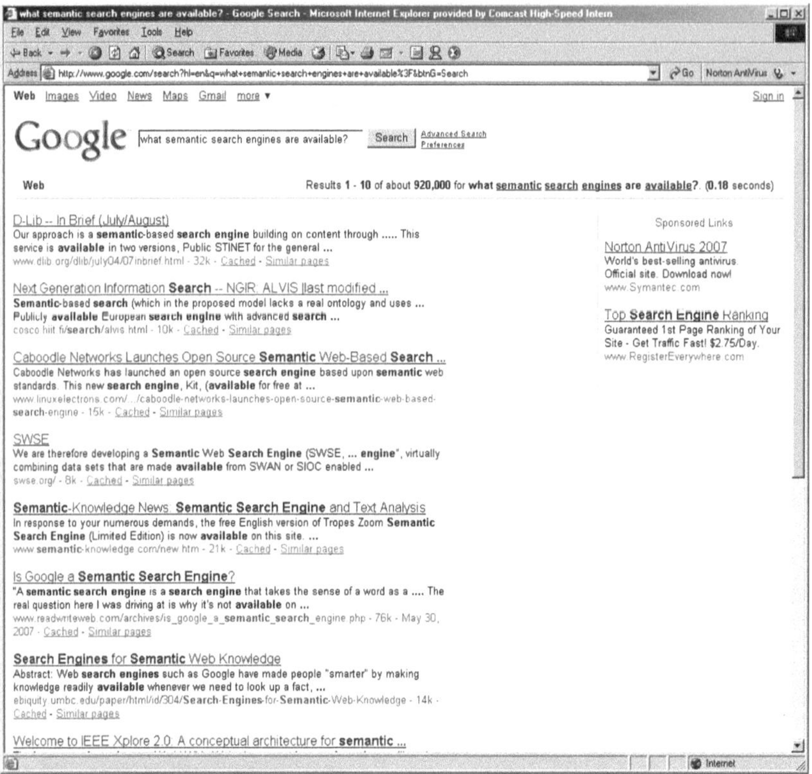

Source: *http://www.google.com*

search engines work and have become accustomed to the process of identifying the appropriate keywords (which may sometimes seem like a secret code), then crossing their fingers in hopes that they will find matching keywords in a document or website. People are more flexible and adaptable than software tools, so they do the adapting. Users transform their query from a question into *search-engine speak*. We are trained to start a search by translating our query into keywords; it has become second nature for us to use this indirect approach to asking a question. What if we could skip the translation,

Figure 2.3 Yahoo! result for search 'sell semantic OR semantically OR semantics "search engine"'

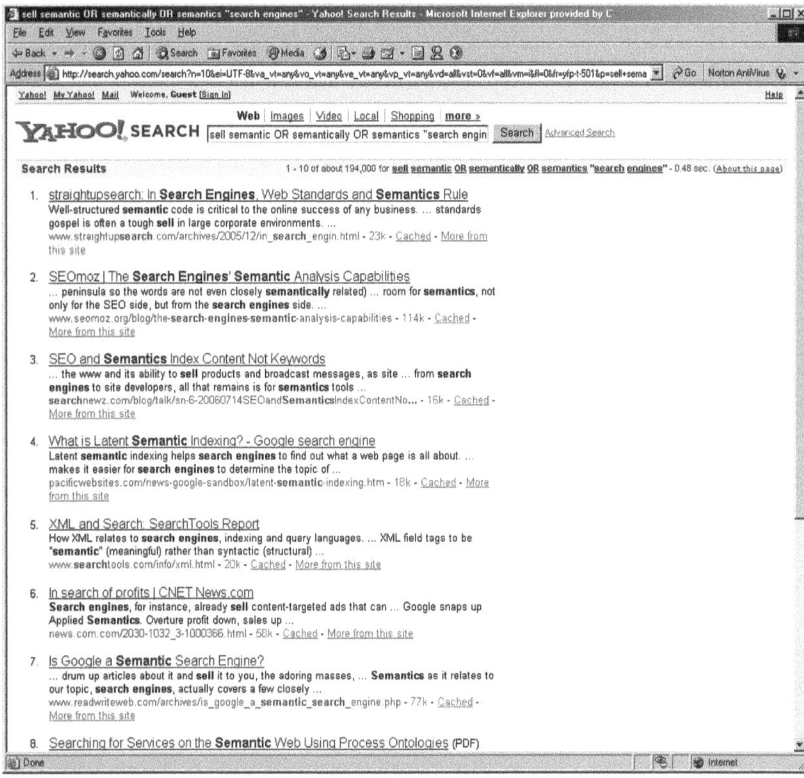

Source: *http://search.yahoo.com*

eliminate the brainstorming for additional keywords, and just enter the question in plain English, like we tried with the first search approach? 'What semantic search engines are currently available?' Think of the time and frustration we would save!

Which of the results you receive are relevant?

In search terms, the concept of precision means that the results you receive match precisely the information you seek. Although this is to some degree an elaboration on the previous section, the question we explore here is 'In what order should the results be presented?'. The order in which results are displayed by a search engine is determined by its 'ranking algorithm', the formula which generally uses a basic scoring mechanism to decide which results should be at the top of the list.

A Pew report states that the average user views 1.9 pages of results per search (Fallows, 2005), which makes it very important that the most relevant information appears on the first few pages of the results list. This fact has given rise to new marketing strategies such as Search Engine Optimization (SEO) that help companies keep their listing at the top of the search rankings. Although Google keeps its ranking algorithm confidential, other companies are open about how their search results are ranked. Some engines use a popularity model, where the web pages ranked highest are the ones that are referenced by the largest number of other web pages.

Teoma (the search engine behind Ask.com) uses an authority-based ranking algorithm, where the pages that are cited by the largest number of *authoritative* websites will appear at the top of your search results. Ranking by authority can produce interesting results; folklore tells of two people who commented on an online article: a person who claimed to be the second coming of Zeus and a Yale professor with impressive credentials; the comments of the former appeared higher on the results list for the ranking algorithms. Apparently Zeus outranked Yale.

Are any of these ranking methods a sure way of getting the most relevant results?

How do you know whether the search engine missed anything important?

In search technology circles, the extent to which a search engine provides complete results is termed 'recall'. In some cases, you need what is called 'total recall', a list of absolutely everything that exists that meets your search criteria. If you are considering putting a significant amount of money into a biotechnology company and need to ensure a return on your investment, you will need to know all other competing products that exist. If you hope to determine whether an idea has already been patented, you need to identify all information that resembles your work and might be considered 'prior art'. In these cases, total recall is critical. In other cases, the amount of recall is not critical at all. When looking for a local restaurant, if your search results do not include every local restaurant, you will likely still be satisfied with your choices. Getting a subset of the restaurants that meet your criteria is adequate.

Consider another example: if you search for *heart attack*, you will find web pages that mention both words together. If your ranking algorithm is working well, closer to the bottom of your results list you will see pages containing the words heart and attack, but not necessarily next to each other. What you will *not* find is online material that contains the phrases 'myocardial infarction' or 'heart infarction' if that material does not also include the words heart and attack. These are technical terms that a physician or medical professional would use when writing about heart attacks. Web pages and other documents that mention these words would definitely be relevant to your search but are not captured because of matching based only on text, not on concept. This inability of search engines to return results that contain synonyms in addition to the exact keywords you specify is a serious liability of text matching systems. To address this liability, most researchers today will continue editing their query to include as many synonyms as possible until they are satisfied that they have found everything that is relevant.

Some search engines have begun using semantics by creating synonym lists and returning results by searching for synonyms of keywords. This addresses the issue regarding a search for *heart attack* above, as long as the engine has included *myocardial infarction* and *heart infarction* as two expressions in the synonym list. But have experts been used to create the synonym lists? Is the list complete and up to date? Many synonym lists in use today are severely limited in scope. The task of maintaining these lists to keep them updated with terms used in current literature, as well as preserving the previously used terms, is an important and significant endeavor that applies to the creation of ontologies as well.

What does semantic search have to offer?

Semantic search allows users to express questions in a natural way, rather than forcing them to translate their information needs into a combination of keywords. By taking meaning into consideration and searching for concepts or ideas, not just keywords, semantic search provides better precision and recall. Before addressing the main question of this chapter, how semantic search works, let us first explore several techniques for extracting meaning.

Semantic techniques

Natural language processing

A natural language is any language used to communicate among individuals. Natural language processing (NLP) is the field of computer science which deals with interpreting natural language; it is the study of how words are strung together to convey meaning. Natural language parsing is the process of deciphering a natural language, of breaking it into parts so that its meaning may be recognized. There are many software programs available to accomplish this task; most output a simple representation of the sentence which, when presented visually, looks a bit like the sentence diagrams that most of us completed in grade school. To diagram a sentence, look first for the nouns, verbs, and objects, and place them on a horizontal line. A vertical line through the horizontal line is placed between subject and verb. Then a vertical line stopping at the horizontal line is placed between verb and object. Modifiers are placed on diagonal lines below the word they modify. For example, the sentence 'The teacher had ten silly students' can be diagrammed as shown in Figure 2.4.

Though this example is for a simple sentence, the same process can be used for a much longer and more complicated expression. See Figure 2.5, which represents the first sentence of the Gettysburg Address.

Figure 2.4 Diagram of the sentence 'The teacher had ten silly students'

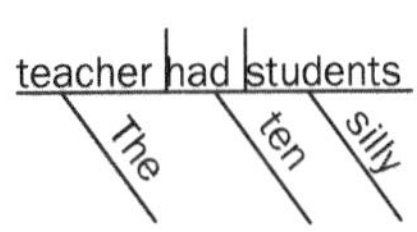

Figure 2.5 Diagram of the first sentence of the Gettysburg Address

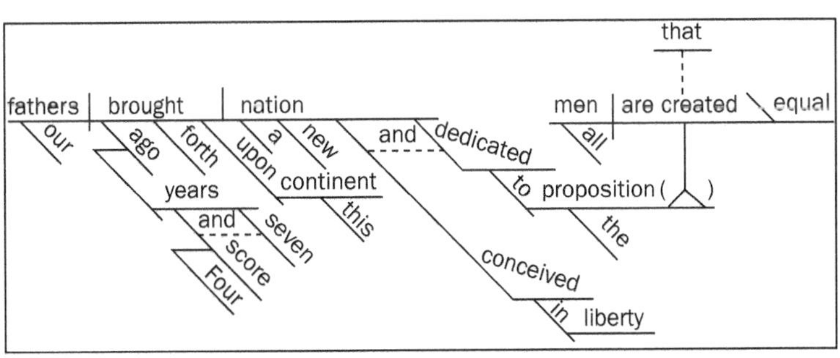

Source: Moutoux, 2008; *http:// www.geocities.com/gene_moutoux/gettysburg1.htm*

Semantic analysis

Diagramming sentences can help us to understand the meaning of a sentence. From Figure 2.5, one might determine that the most important concepts are:

- Fathers brought nation
- Men are created equal

Diagramming a sentence and understanding its meaning are not exact sciences. It is possible to diagram the same sentence in different ways and to varying degrees of detail. However, to get the basic idea of a sentence, machines need not make a thorough or detailed sentence diagram. Just as humans do when they listen to one another or read text, machines are capable of getting the main idea of a statement without making a perfect analysis. Automated semantic analysis tools group words together and drop articles and conjunctions to simplify the sentence. The actual output is likely to represent the sentence as a series of subject, verb, and object combinations similar to those shown in Table 2.1.

In a semantic search, NLP and semantic analysis are employed on both sides of the search:

- when the source material is indexed or mined (i.e. the content is processed so that the computer understands what concepts are on the page)
- when the user enters a question in natural language (i.e. the language in the query is processed so that the computer understands what concepts the user is looking for).

At both points, NLP dissects sentences into meaningful parts.

Table 2.1 **Subject, verb, and object combinations**

subject	fathers	men	nation
verb	brought	are created	conceived
object	nation	equal	in liberty

Referencing an ontology

Another important semantic technique is mapping concepts to an ontology. The ontology is created by experts to define the most important concepts and relationships in the area of interest, or *domain*. Once the language of the source (website, document, paragraph, etc.) is processed, those meaningful parts are then matched with a designated ontology to discover domain-specific meaning.

This mapping can be accomplished in a number of ways. Some systems maintain a synonym list by choosing a preferred word or phrase to represent an entire concept. Other systems map lists of words or phrases to a concept identifier. For example, let us say the verb *equal* is represented by the identifier R2. Other variations on this word include equals, equaled, equality, equalize, and so on. In the ontology, these words would all be marked with the same identifier, R2, to represent the concept of equality.

Some ontologies associate a part of speech with a word or phrase to further distinguish concepts. In either case, the representation would look a bit different after the mapping. For example, using our example from the Gettysburg Address and assuming that our ontology contains the concepts and relationships as described in Table 2.2, the representation of the major concepts might look like this: C2 R1 C3. C1 R3 R2. Note that R2 and R3 represent concepts that can either be used as nouns or verbs.

Table 2.2 **Preferred terms of the major concepts in the Gettysburg Address**

Concept or relationship	Preferred term for the concept, followed by other ways of naming the concept
C1	humankind, humans, man, male homo sapiens
C2	father, dad, fatherly, fatherhood, daddy, ...
C3	country, nation, ...
R1	bring, to bring, brings, bringing, brought, fetch, ...
R2	equals, equaled, equality, equalize, ...
R3	create, created, creation, creating, ...

Concepts will be replaced with identifiers or with preferred terms that may render the sentence *grammatically incorrect but semantically equivalent* in terms of our ontology. For example, the machine may render the sentence into 'humankind create country', which is obviously grammatically incorrect. But since all of those terms are semantically equivalent, the machine understands the concepts represented by the sentence. Some semantic search engines will create a collection of queries, using different combinations of synonyms, which then are sent to various text search engines; this is termed a 'federated search'. Others create a semantic index identifying the concepts and relationships represented in a large collection of documents; this content can then be searched semantically.

Ranking the results

The last class of techniques that will be discussed here is ranking. As mentioned above, ranking is a task performed by all search engines to determine in what order the results should be presented to the user. One of the most powerful features of an ontology-based system is that it can rank the results based on the most important concepts that users have identified in their query. Based on the strength of the connection, the results that most closely fit the entire meaning of the question are the ones that will appear at the top. In a sense, the *user* defines the criteria for ranking the results. By mentioning in the query 'all men are created equal' and 'fathers brought nation', material that contains the concepts of 'all men', 'equality', 'fathers', and 'nation' will appear closer to the top of the results list than material that only mentions 'equality'.

The number of times a concept appears in the source text may be a good indicator of a stronger correlation between the query and the source. If the concept of 'equality' (not just the word equality) appears 1,000 times in a 10,000 word document, then it is more strongly connected to the concept than a document that mentions equality 1,000 times in a document 1,000,000 words long. Thus the ratio of occurrences of a concept to the size of the document is another important consideration when results are ranked.

Semantic searching behind the scenes

A number of companies provide semantic search capabilities. Most use some or all of the techniques discussed in the previous section, but implementation varies, as do the ontologies they use and their emphasis on one technique over another.

The Linguamatics I2E (I2E) solution provides data mining, knowledge extraction and search capabilities. I2E captures the concepts and relationships from data sources maintained by the user or the user's company, as well as sources that are commercially or publicly available. Queries may be expressed graphically through a drag and drop interface, as well as in natural language.

CognitionSearch from Cognition Technologies, Inc., began by building a large electronic dictionary and semantic database, which now contains over 536,000 concepts. CognitionSearch employs linguistics and mathematical algorithms, saving context interpretations at indexing time, so that users may present queries in natural language.

The Semantic Knowledge Indexing Platform (SKIP) from Jarg Corporation employs an ontology based on the Unified Medical Language System (UMLS), which contains over 1.3 million health care and biomedical concepts and is maintained by the National Library of Medicine. SKIP provides natural language query processing for queries and source documents. A semantic index is created for the source documents so that the bulk of the hard work is done at the indexing stage rather than at search time. SKIP will be used for demonstration purposes in the remainder of this chapter because it provides a user-friendly diagram to represent how the query was interpreted by the system, making it easier to show how semantic search works.

The first step to enabling semantic search is to create a semantic index for a collection, which is done by analyzing the structure of the text carrying out the following steps:

1. *Analyze the natural language* – First the natural language parser analyzes the content and separates it into sentences. Prepositions and articles are removed and punctuation and conjunctions are used to group the text into meaningful phrases the machine can understand. Subjects, verbs, and objects are identified and assumed to be the most important concepts in the text.
2. *Map the words/phrases to concepts and relationships in the ontology* – Figure 2.6 is produced by SKIP after natural language parsing is completed and references to the ontology have been established; it displays the concept names and relationships that were detected, grouped semantically.

Figure 2.6 Semantic grouping of concept names and relationships for the first sentence of the Gettysburg Address

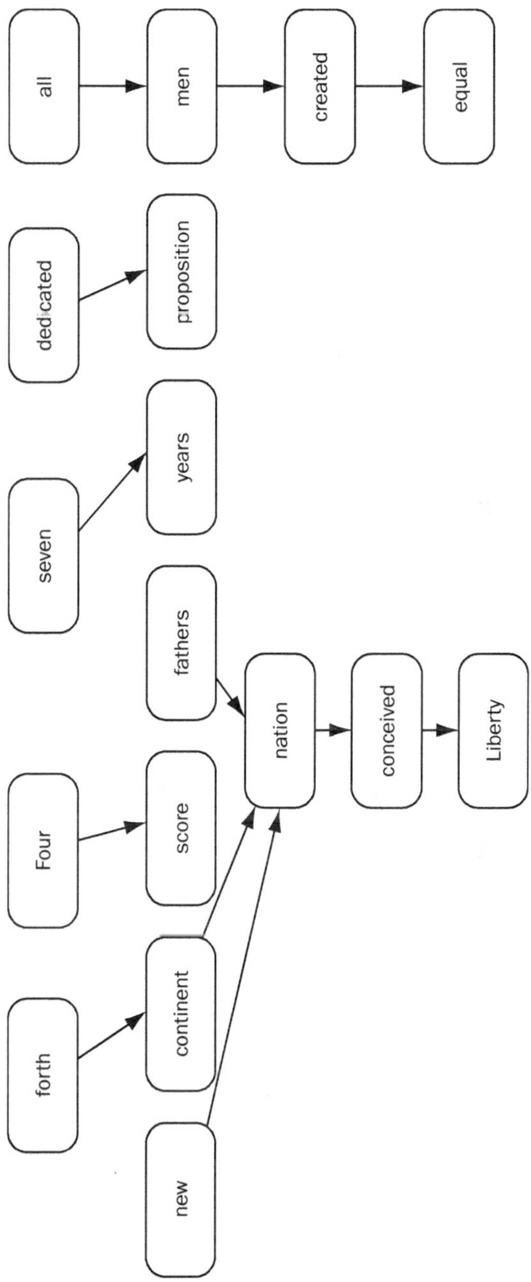

Source: *http://gw.jarg.com*

3. *Create a semantic index* – An index in a book connects a key word or phrase to a page within a document. Similarly, a semantic index connects an idea to a location within a document (which may be as general as a page or as specific as a sentence). The concepts of liberty and equality would map to the first sentence of the Gettysburg Address. Some semantic search engines combine words and relationships to create more complex concepts. For example, the phrase 'all men are created equal' may be mapped to the concept of 'equality' in some systems. Such complex concepts also appear in the semantic index so that searching for complex concepts can occur as quickly as searching for simple ones.

Figure 2.7 **Screenshot of search results for the first sentence of the Gettysburg Address**

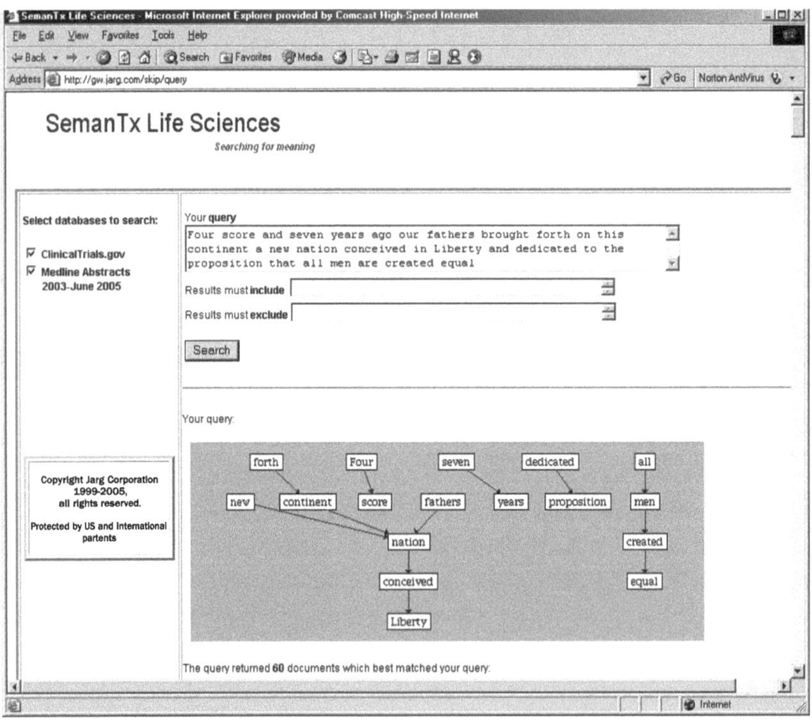

Source: *http://gw.jarg.com*

4. *Query* – Once the source documents are indexed, a user may then enter a question or statement into the system using natural language. Figure 2.7 was taken from the website gw.jarg.com and demonstrates that the same NLP and ontology analysis has been applied to the query as was applied to the source document. This means that the closer the document is to the diagram of this query, the higher it would appear in the results list.
5. *Rank the results* – Results are then ranked according to the criteria set by the user in the question. The SemanTx Life Sciences website has medical literature indexed. Thus, to demonstrate the relevancy ranking, we will attempt a researcher's question: 'What is the role of activins, inhibins, BMP, nodal and MIS-signaling in breast cancer as related to therapeutic targets?' (Figure 2.8).

Figure 2.8 **Screenshot of search 'What is the role of activins, inhibins, BMP, nodal and MIS-signaling in breast cancer as related to therapeutic targets?'**

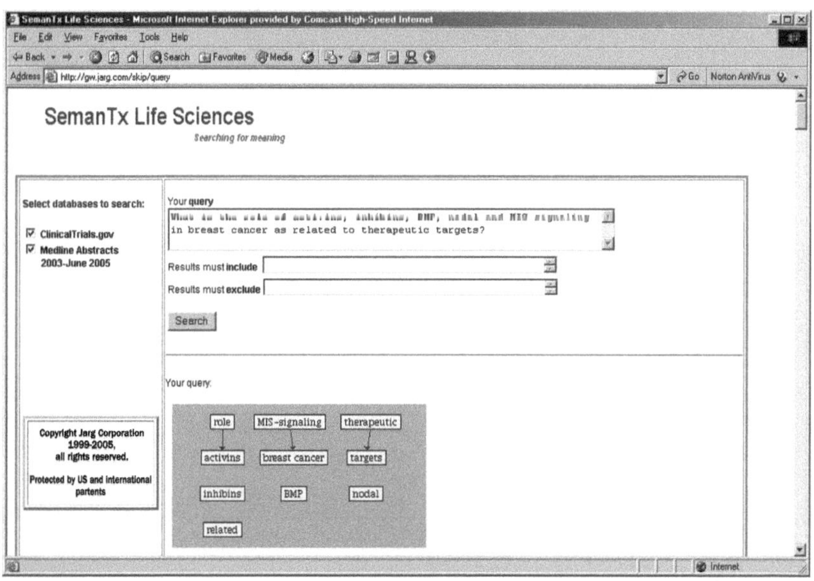

Source: *http://gw.jarg.com*

The sentence diagram in Figure 2.8 sets the criteria for relevancy ranking. The first four results are shown in Figure 2.9; note that by looking at the text map, you can see that the match found in the first document is more complex and more closely matches the query than the other results.

The majority of popular search engines today are based on keyword and text matching. Although users may do their best to choose words that describe the ideas they are looking for, in the end, the search engines are just matching words in the search box to words on web pages and documents. In contrast, semantic search enables the user to search for the concept, not

Figure 2.9 **Screenshot showing first four results of search 'What is the role of activins, inhibins, BMP nodal and MIS-signaling in breast cancer as related to therapeutic targets?'**

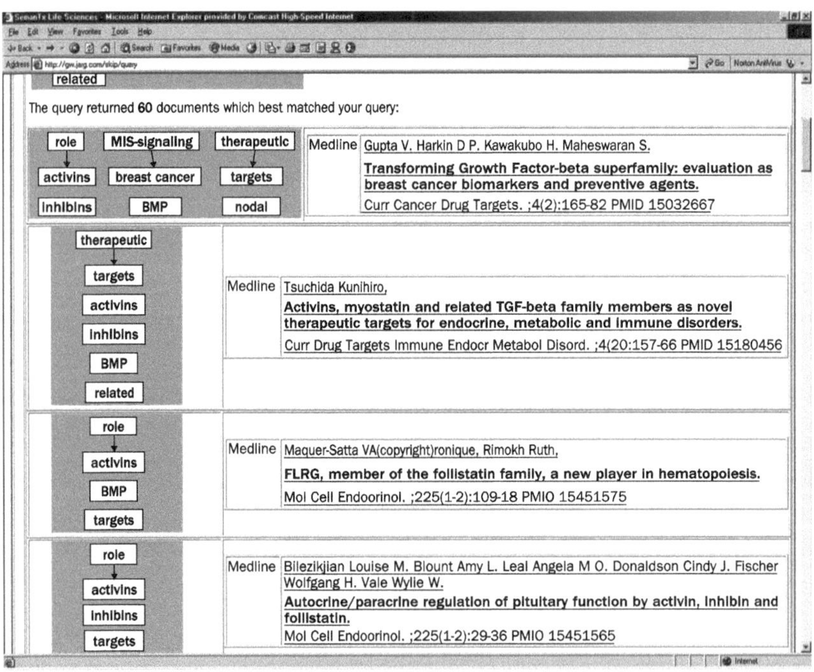

Source: *http://gw.jarg.com*

just the word. This powerful capability erases any doubts about relevance because it allows users to express their information needs easily, to be assured that the results they receive are relevant, and to know that the search engine retrieved everything that is important based on the user's criteria.

Key concepts

- *Keyword search* is generally a trial and error process where users search for one set of keywords, review the results and continually modify the search criteria until they either give up or find enough information.
- *Semantic technologies* allow users to communicate in more natural ways – in plain English.
- Recall, precision, and ranking determine whether a search is effective. Depending on your search needs, one may be more or less important than the other. *Recall* indicates the completeness of the results: Have you found everything that meets your search criteria? *Precision* describes how well the results meet your search criteria. *Ranking* refers to the order in which results are presented. Some search engines use statistical means to determine the order; semantic search engines use a measure of relevance.
- *Natural language parsing* or processing (NLP) is the process of deciphering a natural language, of breaking it into parts so that its meaning may be recognized. This is also called *syntactic analysis*.
- *Semantic analysis* is the process of associating meaning to the output of the syntactic analysis.
- *Semantic search* enables the user to search for a concept of meaning, not just words.

- A *semantic search engine* might:
  - process the documents by:
    - carrying out NLP to generate a syntactic description (sentence diagram)
    - carrying out semantic analysis to compare the sentence diagram to an ontology, to identify the concepts represented in the document
    - creating an index of the concepts in each document;
  - process the query by:
    - carrying out NLP
    - carrying out semantic analysis
    - searching the semantic index using concept identifiers
    - ranking results according to the concepts identified in the query.

3

Creating an ontology

As described thus far, ontologies are useful for representing, defining, and arranging the concepts that make up the knowledge of a domain and for understanding the connections between those concepts. We have mentioned different uses for ontologies, such as aiding in the classification of documents, integrating data, or using them to fine tune queries for a search engine, providing better results. Now we will turn our attention to how to construct an ontology. Whether you go on to create one yourself or not, understanding how they are built is critical to understanding their power.

How to create an ontology

This chapter provides an overview of how an ontology is created following a step-by-step example of one used for organizing restaurant reviews. We will see how this ontology evolves from a nebulous group of ideas into an organized web of related concepts representing a specific domain.

Step 1: Decide how your ontology will be used

First, take some time to envision how your ontology will be used by answering three main questions:

- Who is your audience?
- Why will they use this ontology?
- What kinds of questions will they ask?

For our example of an ontology related to restaurant reviews, let us consider these questions and possible answers in turn:

- *Who is your audience?* – The audience consists of adults from the general public looking to dine in the Boston area, and restaurant critics.
- *Why would they use this ontology?* – Users will want to know about elements typically addressed in restaurant reviews such as value, ambiance, location, variety of choices, quality of food, and quality of service.
- *What kinds of questions might they ask?*
  - Which restaurant serves the best grilled cheese in Boston?
  - Where in Andover can I get crème brûlée for under $7?
  - Is there a Mexican restaurant with a roof deck near zip code 02115?
  - Which sushi bar in Brookline has the largest menu for the best price?

Step 2: Gather terms related to your domain

Gathering terms related to your domain can be accomplished by several methods, or by combining the methods to create a list that encompasses the breadth and depth of the topic. However, the list you create at this point for any ontology can be short – approximately 50 terms total. The idea here is to generate enough terms to think about categories without having so many terms that you are overwhelmed. The list of terms will be added to and altered after a hierarchy of categories is established.

One way to create this short list is through a classic brainstorming approach. Start with the questions above, a blank piece of paper or a new word-processing document, and just begin with a free flow of words related to your topic, in this case, restaurant reviews. You may wish to do this on your own or with a group of people. Here is a short list of words related to restaurant reviews: Zagat, Service, Waiters, Seating, Noise, Drinks, Pasta, Salad, Meat, Steakhouse, Candlelight, Flowers, Bartender.

Another option for gathering terms is to read a few articles representative of your domain and underline the nouns; these most often help to identify categories or concepts that should be represented in your ontology. You could approach the selection of these articles by choosing documents from a few different points in time, by intentionally aiming for a variety of topics within your domain, or by using some classic often-cited documents that represent core concepts in the area of knowledge. For example, if your ontology was about cooking, including samples of writing by Betty Crocker, Julia Child, or James Beard would turn up a variety of core terms. If you were creating a women's studies ontology, excerpts from Simone de Beauvoir, Betty Friedan, or Gloria Steinem would present a gold-mine of terms for your consideration.

In the case of our example ontology, we can go straight to the source and examine the ideas in a paragraph from a restaurant review:

> But you do not have to like seafood to enjoy Joe Forte's Restaurant. From Grilled Rack of Pork Ribs to

> a custom, hand-cut steak in the size you want, you have plenty of menu options. But do save room for their spectacular desserts. How could you pass up Maple Walnut Baked Alaska, freshly made sorbets or the Decadence Platter for Two. While it may be nice to be tucked away in a cozy booth, it is also fun to experience the American brasserie atmosphere at the massive horseshoe bar – or even dine in the more intimate upstairs and look down on all the action. And, in summer, the Joe's Roof Garden is a pleasant natural setting. (Carr, 2007)

At this point we are attempting to define a common vocabulary so have eliminated proper nouns. Our term list from this exercise might consist of: Seafood, Pork Ribs, Steak, Menu Options, Desserts, Baked Alaska, Sorbets, Platter, Booth, Atmosphere, Bar, Garden, Setting.

Whichever method you choose to gather terms, you will want to create a list of a manageable size during this step so that you do not get overwhelmed by grouping them into categories in Step 3.

Step 3: Create a taxonomy

The third step is to create a taxonomy – a hierarchy of categories. Organizing knowledge hierarchically is a natural process, especially for librarians, when we think about grouping terms into categories. The Library of Congress (LC) and Dewey Decimal Classification systems are both hierarchies, and it is a librarian's role to classify material into the most specific category possible. Figure 3.1 shows examples of the hierarchies in these systems that one would use to catalog or categorize a book about French grammar.

Figure 3.1 **Examples of hierarchies in Dewey and LC categorizing a book about French grammar**

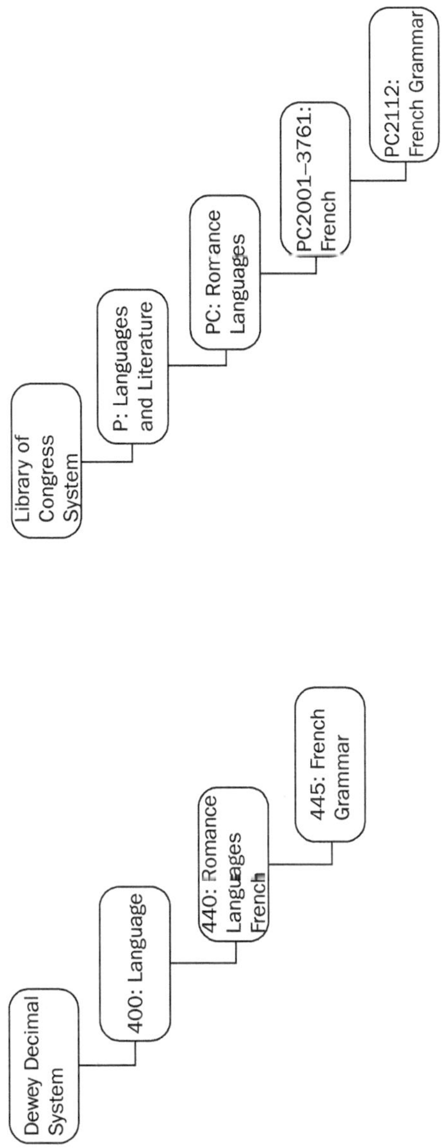

In each case, the librarian works from general to specific, classifying the object with a number and/or letter that designates it not only as a member of its most specific category, but as a member of all the categories above it. In the end, books that share more numbers and letters are more similar than those that share fewer. This is the same case in another taxonomy we are all familiar with – the scientific classification system (Figure 3.2).

Every plant and animal known to man is classified using this system. As flora and fauna are placed into these categories, one can see the extent of similarity between two different species by noting how many of the previous categories they share. For example, species that have the same family but a different genus are more alike than species that have the same class but not the same order.

Figure 3.2 Main classes in the scientific classification system

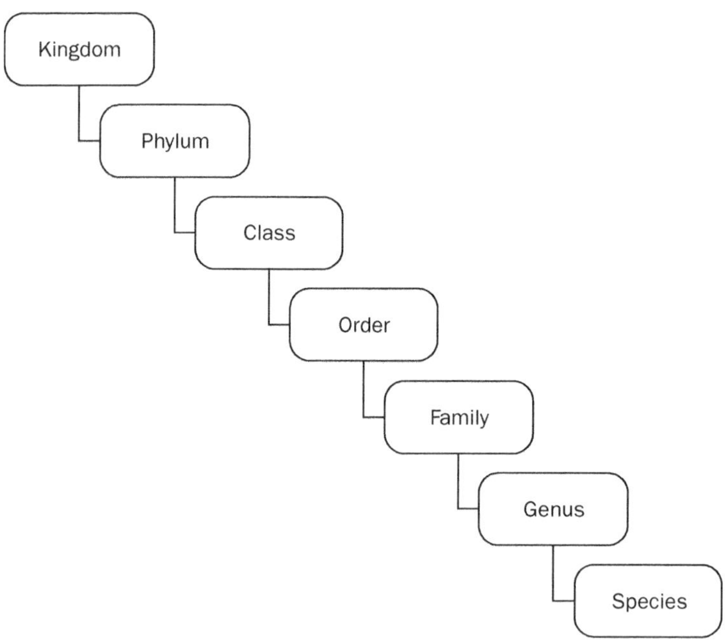

The goal in this step is to define categories that classify the objects in your domain. You will want to look at the list of terms you have created in Step 2 and see what kinds of broad groupings they fit into. One consideration is that often less is more. You may only need ten categories to accommodate your list. You may need to allow for more specificity by creating 20 categories. Depending on the size of your list, the reason you are creating it, and the structure of knowledge in a particular domain, your taxonomy will vary in size. But do consider that categories should be broad enough to accommodate a variety of similar ideas. The relationships between those ideas will be specified at a later time.

In thinking about restaurants reviews and the kinds of information they contain, ratings and reviews seem to focus on three aspects: setting, service, and fare. These categories can be further broken down as illustrated in Figure 3.3.

Now that we have established a basic structure of categories, we can see whether these broad groupings would

Figure 3.3 **Different categories within a restaurant review**

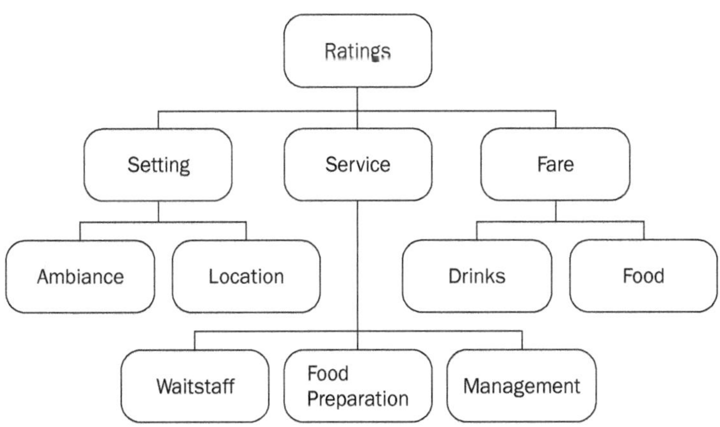

accommodate the list of terms generated previously or whether further modifications need to be made. While some terms may fit into more than one category, for purposes of simplicity you will want to choose just one category for each. Some terms may not yet fit into a category and may be placed in a 'miscellaneous' category for the time being. Here is our list of terms and the categories that they would fit into according to Figure 3.3:

- *Setting* – Ambiance: Seating, Noise, Candlelight, Flowers, Booth, Atmosphere, Bar, Garden
- *Service* – Waitstaff: Waiters, Bartender
- *Fare* – Food: Pasta, Salad, Meat, Seafood, Pork Ribs, Desserts, Steak, Baked Alaska, Sorbets
- *Ratings* – Restaurant Guides: Zagat
- *Miscellaneous* – Steakhouse, Menu Options, Platter.

We notice immediately that in the Food category, we can arrange the terms into a hierarchy of their own using just the terms given. Pork Ribs and Steak are kinds of Meat. Baked Alaska and Sorbets are kinds of Desserts. These examples suggest that we create another level of categories to accommodate these shared characteristics. Figure 3.4 illustrates how these categories can be broken down further.

Now the Pork Ribs can be classified as a type of Pork, which is a type of Meat dish, which is a type of Main Course, which is a type of Food, which is a type of Fare. In ontology building, this relationship is appropriately known as a subclass or the 'is_a' relationship, when one term 'is a type of' another term. All terms placed within a category share characteristics inherent both to the immediate category and all categories previous to it. By placing a term as a member of a category, you are acknowledging that the term is

Figure 3.4 **Further breakdown of categories within a restaurant review**

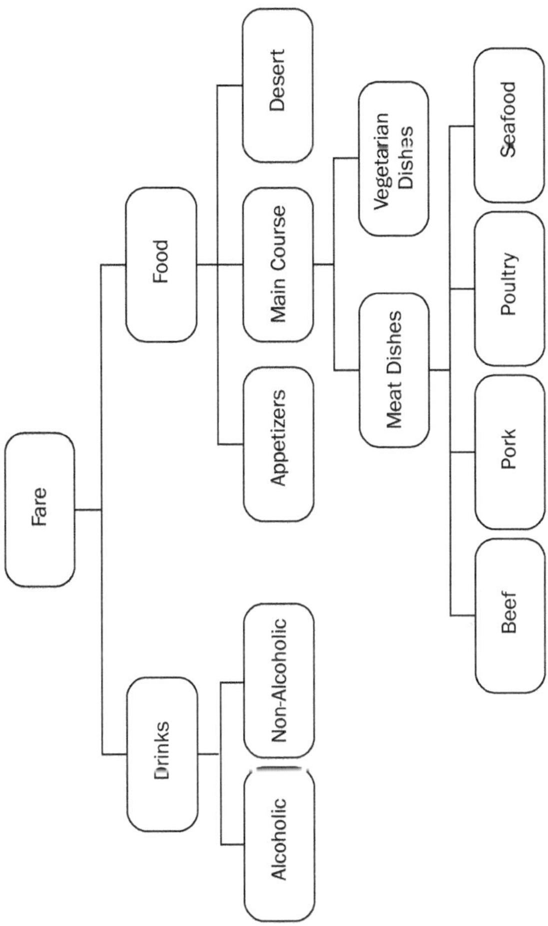

a subset of all of those groups. In the language of ontologies, our terms would look like this:

> Pork is_a Meat Dish
> Meat Dish is_a Main Course
> Main Course is_a Food

These 'is_a' relationships are the organizing principle behind the notion of a taxonomy and are the most common relationships found in an ontology. Other relationships aside from these 'parent–child' relationships will be established in Step 7.

Additionally, by adding the categories Dessert and Vegetarian Dishes in this expansion of the model, we have created places for Baked Alaska, Sorbets, Pasta, and Salad.

No matter how you choose to arrange your categories you will need to define what each category contains so that you can easily place terms into the taxonomy. By having a statement of what the category will include you will be able to tell when a term belongs (and just as importantly does *not* belong) in a particular group. Here are examples of definitions for a few of the categories above:

- Fare – includes any consumable item found at a restaurant
- Drinks – includes any beverage available at a restaurant
- Food – includes any non-beverage consumable items available at a restaurant
- Beef – includes any meat originally from a cow
- Poultry – includes any meat originally from a chicken, turkey, duck, or goose.

Now that these definitions are set, other terms can be generated and placed in categories according to the established descriptions.

Step 4: Add more terms to each category

As you look at these categories and their definitions new terms probably come to mind in each group. There are a number of ways you could develop this list further: by using a previously established term list, by examining relevant documents in your discipline, or by brainstorming.

The same techniques mentioned in Step 1 work here as well. In developing a restaurant ontology one might consider looking at a Zagat survey, which offers listings and reviews for eating establishments. Even the phone book's listing of local restaurants might present you with options for new terms to add.

Obviously each of these categories could have hundreds of terms and you may determine that some actually constitute categories rather than individual terms. As you add terms, always come back to the answers you established in Step 1 to determine if you are still on the right track: Who is your audience? Why will they use this search engine? What kinds of questions will they ask? If the information you are adding does not seem relevant to these answers, you probably do not need to add it.

Step 5: Define terms

Defining terms is a critical step because it is where the domain-specific context is provided. The meanings of the terms here are dictated by the domain. If you look at any dictionary entry, you will see that most words have more than one definition, more than one sense of the word. Think of this step as the ability to craft your own dictionary, choosing the sense of each word that most closely fits how your domain uses it.

In our example, we are using the ontology as the basis for natural language analysis for a semantic search engine, so each term's definition will be used by the natural language processor to map both the text of the source documents and the text of users' queries. The definitions will provide the basis for matching the documents to the queries and providing relevant results.

You can construct the best definitions with a combination of adaptation from reference books and conversations with subject matter experts. Speaking with experts is crucial since incorporating human experience largely makes up the value of an ontology. This is a time-consuming process but it makes the difference between a general dictionary and a domain-specific knowledge structure.

To continue with our restaurant review ontology, let us take the example of the term Bar, which has varied definitions, including: the bar examination required of lawyers; a piece of wood mounted on a wall for ballet dancers; the metal bars on a jail cell and so on. In this step, you establish that the bar related to your purpose is both a counter where drinks are served inside a restaurant, as well as a general term for an establishment serving alcohol.

Step 6: Add synonyms

Adding synonyms, or 'other names', to the terms is what turns them from single words into representations of concepts. Think of this step as turning a dictionary into a thesaurus. You are taking one idea and coming up with all the different names for it. In this way you will be enabling the user to ask questions in their own language since all of the similar names for a term will be cross referenced by relationships.

Taking our example ontology through this step, your role would be to come up with words and phrases that other people would think of when searching for information about a particular term. A user might query 'Where are the best waiters in Boston?' while a review might mention an experience with a particular 'server'. You would want to establish an equal relationship between the two terms so that the search engine would present that particular review as a result. This relationship would be expressed as:

Waiter other_name Server

The advantage of this synonym list is that the burden of remembering all the different ways of naming a 'waiter' rests with the computer rather than the user. The user will not have to think about all the possible ways to express the same concept and will not need to spend time using a trial and error approach to get the right combination of synonyms in order to describe her information need.

Step 7: Define relationships and use them to connect terms

This final step of adding relationships is what separates the structures we already know – a dictionary, thesaurus, and taxonomy – from an ontology. This is the crucial point where your knowledge structure turns from a linear model of terms and categories into a web of ideas. These relationships will serve the purpose of connecting any two terms in your vocabulary. This pattern of one term connected through a relationship to another term is called a triple and always follows the structure: Term Relationship Term, or put another way: Subject Verb Object.

You will want to think about the kinds of relationships that it will be important to establish between terms. In the restaurant review example, relationships should express:

- *actions* such as performed_by, caused_by, managed_by, interacts_with

- *locations* such as adjacent_to, connected_to, has_location
- *conceptual connections* such as consists_of, ingredient_of, version_of.

Action relationships will be most relevant to how service is carried out and how food is prepared. Location relationships will be most relevant to which part of the state each restaurant is in. Conceptual connection relationships will be most relevant to ingredients in recipes.

Other important ideas are:

- how food is prepared (ingredient_of, consists_of, has_form, cooked_with)
- how food is served (served_by, served_with, served_on)
- the hierarchy and interaction of staff (managed_by, works_with)
- the quality of the atmosphere (arranged_with, lit_by).

We will need to formally define these relationships within the ontology before we can apply them. For example, let us take the relationship 'served_by'. An appropriate definition is 'the act of a customer receiving requested food or drink from a restaurant employee'. We can then use this definition to connect terms in our vocabulary, for example:

> Drinks served_by Bartender
> Desserts served_by Waiter

Once you have established the definitions for relationships, you can create connections between terms. You can move beyond the 'parent–child' relationship inherent in taxonomies and create connections between any two terms, no matter which categories they are in. In the above examples, Waiters and Bartenders are in the category Waitstaff, while Drinks and Desserts are in the category Fare. These connections create the web of knowledge that will allow users the flexibility to ask questions and receive relevant results, regardless of how those questions are phrased.

Step 8: Verify your ontology

Now that you have created a web of concepts, you will need to verify that it works for the purpose you outlined. In the case of the restaurant review ontology, the goal is to use the ontology as a structure on which a natural language search engine can be built. In order to find out if the ontology works, ask colleagues and friends for use-case scenarios – what kinds of questions would they want answers to before making a decision about where to eat? Use these queries, exactly as they were phrased by your colleagues and friends, to figure out whether the ontology represents the meaning behind their questions. Here are examples of some questions they might pose, along with the resulting considerations for your ontology:

'Where is there a vegetarian restaurant accessible by public transportation?'

- Are restaurants classified by whether they are vegetarian or not?
- Is public transportation represented? Is it a category or a relationship?

'Are there any five-star restaurants that offer online reservations?'

- Are different rating systems represented?
- If one reviewer assigns ratings with fork icons instead of stars, are those ideas connected?
- Is there a way to indicate whether a restaurant offers online reservations? Or whether they take reservations at all?

Another step in verification is making sure that all relationships are mutual, meaning that the relationship is expressed both backward and forward, and that all mutual relationships hold true. If A is a parent of B, then the opposite relationship should also be expressed: B is a child of A. In our example, we would need to ensure that these relationships are expressed in both ways, and that they are accurate:

> Drinks served_by Bartender
> Bartender serves Drinks

Step 9: Revise

It is often said in librarianship that the nature of bibliography is that it never ends, changing and growing as new literature is published and new research changes how previous work is interpreted. The same holds true for the nature of ontology: it will change and grow as your domain takes shape. Developing an ontology is an iterative process. You should expect dramatic changes while carrying out the steps demonstrated above, and hopefully many fewer and less dramatic changes after the ontology is in use. At that point, though, you should include a feedback mechanism so that you can determine whether users are finding what they need. If not, there may be obvious and simple changes you can make to the ontology to improve search results.

Although the creation and maintenance of an ontology is time-intensive at the beginning, once the main structure is laid out, you will only need to make small changes in order to affect the retrieval of information. In traditional indexing and cataloging, a new subject heading or keyword can make it necessary to review mean reviewing thousands of documents to see if those headings apply to previously indexed documents. With an ontology, once new vocabulary enters the lexicon or new research shows a previously unestablished connection, these changes can be made quickly and in one place in the ontology to affect all current and future knowledge in your system.

Key concepts

Creating an ontology involves the following tasks:

- *Define the goals* of the ontology – How will your ontology be used? Who is your audience? What questions will they ask?
- *Identify core terms* – Using a sample set of data, begin to identify the most important vocabulary in your domain.
- *Create a taxonomy* – Organize the important terms into hierarchical categories.
- *Add terms to the taxonomy* – Review the existing terms and categories to help to identify missing terms.
- *Define terms* – Identify the sense of the term as it relates to your domain.
- *Add synonyms* – Document other ways of representing the same idea.
- *Define relationships and use them to make connections* – Document how each term relates to other terms.

- *Verify the ontology by selecting another sample set of data* – Explore use-case scenarios to see if any important terms or categories are missing.
- *Revise* – As the ontology is used in real-life scenarios and the domain progresses, collect user feedback and establish new terms, categories, and relationships to make improvements.

4

Building an ontology from existing components

In the previous chapter, we demonstrated how to build an ontology from the ground up, which is a significant undertaking in any situation. Another approach to building an ontology is to start with an existing knowledge structure, such as a taxonomy, a thesaurus, or an existing ontology, and customize it for your domain and your purpose. In an existing knowledge structure, the basic concepts are already established, in many cases complete with definitions, synonyms, and hierarchies. Your effort would be entirely dedicated to building on what exists already to create an ontology representative of your domain.

In some cases, though, you may discover that the customization is more labor-intensive than beginning from scratch. Thus the first few steps of evaluating your needs and the available resources are critical in deciding whether a ground-up or customization approach will work best for your needs.

Choosing components

As librarians we are familiar with a number of well-established classification schemes, the most obvious being the

Library of Congress and Dewey Decimal Classification systems. But many subject areas also have their own thesauri. The Educational Research Information Center (ERIC) publishes the *Thesaurus of ERIC Descriptors*. The American Psychological Association maintains the *Thesaurus of Psychological Index Terms*. Other disciplines such as agriculture, politics, and technology all have their own thesauri as well. If you start with a thesaurus such as one of these, your ontology construction would be partially finished leaving you to focus only on arranging the terms into hierarchies and establishing more specific relationships between concepts.

Other data sources could be useful, too, such as an existing taxonomy, perhaps even one that you have used already. Taxonomies define the categories for an ontology. First, determine whether it would make sense to use the entire taxonomy or just the portion of the taxonomy that provides the best match of categories to the concepts of your domain. While you will still need to add definitions, synonyms, and relationships to transform a taxonomy into an ontology, it can be very helpful to have the categories pre-defined.

Or you could turn to non-academic sources that provide more commonly used categories or concepts. One example is the categories found in the *Yellow Pages*, which could be used as a starting point for an ontology about consumer products. Alternatively, the *North American Product Classification System*, produced by the US Census Bureau, defines products for many industries. For example, the product list for finance and insurance contains definitions for consumer loans, construction mortgages, foreign currency, and overdraft protection (US Census Bureau, 2007). These product lists include clear definitions and cross references to related data.

Another possibility is to start with an existing ontology (there are many available), which already contains relevant concepts, relationships, and categories, and dedicate your effort to adding terms from your domain and establishing new relationships from the point of view of your domain or subject area.

When you select an ontology as a starting point, consider its size and complexity. A disadvantage of using a large ontology is that it has many concepts and relationships to examine; it may require an automated tool which can compare literature from your domain to the ontology in order to identify missing categories and concepts. You may also need to examine the existing concepts and relationships for inconsistencies and inaccuracies. The best strategy is to find the smallest, best organized ontology that provides a good match for what you need. We will explore the process of extending an existing ontology in the Center on Media and Child Health case study in Part 3, Chapter 9. In the current chapter, we will take an existing recipe taxonomy and transform it into an ontology.

Customizing your knowledge structure

Let us follow an example, taking an existing knowledge structure from its base to an ontology, customizing as we go. Imagine that you have been hired by a culinary institute to create an ontology representing all of the recipes they use while teaching their students. Since the basic steps of creating an ontology are the same whether we start from scratch or from an existing knowledge source, we will follow the steps outlined in Chapter 3.

Step 1: Decide how your ontology will be used

Through speaking with the staff at the culinary institute, you have answered these questions:

- *Who is your audience?* – Students and staff of the culinary institute
- *Why will they use this ontology?* – For a semantic search engine where they can ask and learn about recipes taught in classes
- *What kinds of questions will they ask?*
  - Which recipes include wine as an ingredient?
  - What are some common substitutes for vegetable oil in baking?
  - Which vegetarian recipes have ingredients similar to those in chicken piccatta?
  - Does any Mexican appetizer or main dish chicken recipe use a tablespoon or more of cilantro?

Step 2: Gather terms related to your domain

As mentioned in the previous chapter, identifying and defining approximately 50 terms is a manageable task. Whether you are searching for an existing taxonomy, thesaurus, or ontology, you will want to find a source that contains these terms or closely related terms.

Since we are creating an ontology specifically for the culinary institute, we will need to use concepts gathered directly from the institute's recipe books. After looking through their files, we see that terms include: coq au vin, boeuf bourguignon, beef stew, spinach omelet, enchiladas, Caesar salad, potatoes au gratin, and pumpkin pie.

Step 3: Create a taxonomy

Now that we have an idea of the kinds of terms we are looking for, we can start to examine original sources to find one whose structure we could adopt. We could start by looking at different cookbooks to see how they are structured. Is the book organized by when the dish is served during the meal (appetizers, main dish, desserts)? Or by the main ingredient (chicken, beef, fish)? Or by the amount of cooking time (no-cook recipes, 30-minute recipes, 60-minute + recipes)? Review the goals of these cookbooks and compare them to your own goal.

For most cookbooks, the goal is not to have people read from start to finish, but rather to provide easy access to recipes fitting certain characteristics such as being a particular part of a meal, containing a specific ingredient, or being cooked in a certain amount of time. The catch is, with a book, the recipes can only be organized *one* of these ways. They may be able to be cross-referenced in an index, but the layout itself is static and final. In an electronic source, we have the ability to make a knowledge structure that will be versatile enough for students to find recipes based on any of these themes. Perhaps using the organizational structure of a cookbook is not ideal for this project then; perhaps starting with an electronic source more closely resembles the structure we are aiming for.

Turning to the web, there are a number of recipe websites available on which we could base our ontology. For our example, we will look further at *http://www.allrecipes.com*, which contains over 40,000 recipes along with user reviews and ratings. The advantage of electronic data is that it can be organized on the fly, depending on how the user prefers to browse. In addition to their search engine, *http://www.allrecipes.com* has a sidebar where users can browse by course, by ingredient, by cooking method, by occasion, or by cooking style. Under each of these options, there is a list of main groupings for that category; clicking on each of them brings you to a list where you can choose an even smaller subset. This is an indication of an underlying taxonomy. Let us explore how to use this taxonomy as the original source for the recipe ontology.

You will need to examine the relevance of your subject to the existing taxonomy. Would adding your list of terms (in this case, recipes from the school) require redefining categories or increasing the size of the category list significantly? If you are still evaluating multiple sources, eliminate those that would require significant effort to revise; this indicates a poor fit for your domain. Let us examine the existing taxonomic structure at *http://www.allrecipes.com*. Choosing 'Browse by Course' we can see the structure shown in Figure 4.1.

From there, the categories continue to split. For example, Figure 4.2 shows the locations of recipes for chili and nachos.

Since we can see the basic structure available for terms, we can look at those we identified in Step 2 and see whether and where they would fit into the taxonomy:

Main dish – gourmet – poultry – coq au vin
Main dish – gourmet – beef – boeuf bourguignon
Soups, stews and chili – stews – beef stew
Breakfast and brunch – egg dishes – spinach omelet
Main dish – tacos, burritos and enchiladas – enchiladas
Salads – green salads – Caesar salad
Side dish – potatoes – potatoes au gratin
Desserts – pies – custard and cream pies – pumpkin pie

It looks as if most of our terms would fit into the *Allrecipes* taxonomy without the need for too much revision, so we will proceed to use this taxonomy as the base structure for our ontology.

Figure 4.1 **Representation of categories structure on the Allrecipes website**

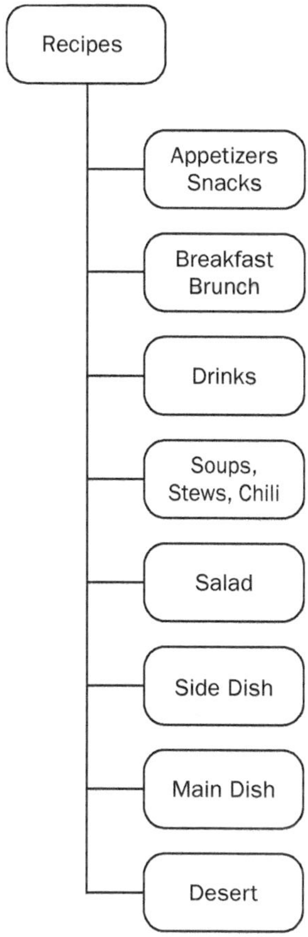

Source: *http://allrecipes.com*

Step 4: Add more terms to each category

In the previous chapter, we suggested generating other terms to add to each category by using a previously established term list, by examining relevant documents in your discipline, or by brainstorming. In this example, since we are using the recipes of the school, we can rely mainly on those

Figure 4.2 **Representation of locations for chili and nachos on the Allrecipes website**

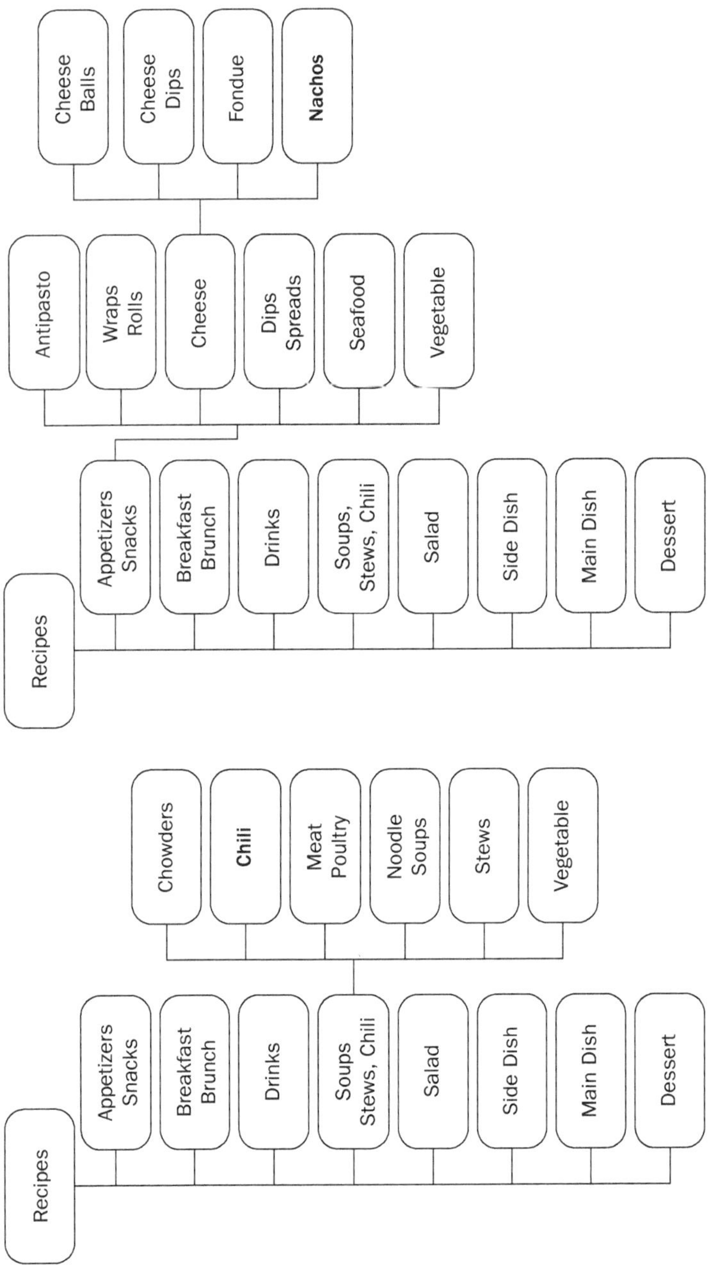

Source: *http://allrecipes.com*

recipes to provide a list of ingredients, units of measure, cooking tools, and other terms mentioned in the instructions. So this step would consist of deciding in which categories to place the given terms rather than focusing on gathering the terms with which to start.

Step 5: Define terms

Defining terms is a critical step because it is where the domain-specific context is provided. A dictionary can be a good place to get ideas for a general definition you can further refine for your subject matter. It is always best to consult with subject experts in order to craft your definitions. In this example, you are working for the culinary school, so you will likely need to involve school staff in this step. Perhaps there is a pastry chef who can clearly explain the difference between pies and tarts, or a French culinary expert who can define the cooking terms that come straight from the French language.

Step 6: Add synonyms

The step of adding synonyms, or 'other names', to the terms is what turns them from single words into representations of concepts. Here are some examples we might encounter in this ontology:

> Scallions other_name Green onions
> Orange rind other_name Orange zest

Note that scallions and green onions are exactly the same thing; they are simply two different names for the same vegetable. You will want to avoid using synonyms to identify items that are really just similar to one another; for example, a vidalia onion and a Spanish onion are two different types of onion with very different flavors so you would not want to link them with the relationship 'other_name', since recipes will clearly call for one or the other.

Step 7: Define relationships and use them to connect terms

As mentioned in the previous chapter, this final step of adding relationships is what separates the structure you have already built from an ontology. This is the crucial point where your knowledge structure turns from being a linear model of terms and categories into a web of ideas. These relationships will serve the purpose of connecting any two terms in your vocabulary.

You will want to think about the kinds of relationships that will be important to establish between terms – which kinds of connections will be necessary for this ontology?:

- *actions* such as performed_by, caused_by, interacts_with
- *locations* such as adjacent_to, connected_to, has_location
- *conceptual connections* such as consists_of, ingredient_of, has_form, version_of

In our culinary ontology example, relationships from two of these categories would be most important: action relationships will be most relevant to how food is prepared and cooked and conceptual connection relationships will be most relevant to ingredients in recipes.

In thinking of what kinds of relationships to establish in this ontology, some important ideas are:

- how food is prepared (chopped_into, has_form, cooked_with)
- how food is cooked (simmered_for, baked_in, grilled_on)

- how food is served (served_with, garnish_for, poured_onto).

First, we will need to define a relationship before we can apply it. For example, let us take the relationship 'baked_in'. An appropriate definition is 'where ingredients are placed to be cooked by dry heat'. We can then use this definition to connect terms in our vocabulary, for example:

> Brownies baked_in 13 x 9 inch metal pan
> Chicken baked_in shallow glass dish

These connections create the web of knowledge that is the essence of ontology building.

Step 8: Verify your ontology

Now that you have created an ontology, you will need to verify that it works for the purpose you outlined. In the case of this culinary institute's ontology, the goal is to use the ontology as a structure on which a semantic search engine can be built. Ask staff and students for use-case scenarios – the kinds of situations in which they would use this tool and the kinds of questions they would want answers to. Here are examples of some queries with the resulting considerations for your ontology:

'What dishes can I make using heavy cream?'

- Are ingredients represented in your ontology?

'Are there any vegetarian recipes similar to duck a l'orange?'

- Is it noted which recipes do not include meat?
- Are ingredients represented so that recipes can be compared?

Step 9: Revise

Using feedback from staff and students, you will be able to find out where your ontology fails to provide adequate information. Then examine areas of the ontology that might explain the failure and aim to improve those areas with either more knowledge or new information. After the basic structure is laid out, you will be able to add new recipes quickly and easily to keep the ontology up to date.

We have now added terms, definitions, and relationships to an existing taxonomy to transform it into an ontology specially suited for the needs of the culinary institute.

Key concepts

- *Building an ontology from existing components* may be a better alternative to creating one from scratch; however, it can also be labor-intensive. Evaluating your needs and the available resources are critical. The most important criterion is how well the existing components capture the vocabulary of the domain.
- The best strategy is to *find the smallest, best organized knowledge source* that provides a good match for what you need.
- The *tasks are the same as for creating an ontology*, but some tasks may be greatly facilitated by your selected knowledge source.

Part 2
Semantic technologies

Although ontologies on their own can provide added value by helping us understand a domain and give a structure for organizing information, their full power is only realized when they are integrated with software tools that exploit the semantic content in ways that are meaningful to the user. Thus, to understand the value of ontologies, it is important to understand the full scope of semantic technologies as well as the integrated tools that will deliver the power of semantics to the user.

Semantic technology commonly includes any automated software tool that processes information based on an interpretation of meaning. Interpretation of meaning may take several forms. One form is the ability to recognize different ways of identifying the same idea. For example, a tool that finds all documents that contain the keyword 'AIDS' does not constitute a semantic technology because this may be implemented by simply matching the pattern of the letters, but a tool that identifies the equivalence of 'AIDS', 'Acquired Immune Deficiency Syndrome', and 'acquired immunodeficiency' could be called a semantic tool. Another form is the ability to identify related concepts such as 'Human Immunodeficiency Virus' and 'AZT'. Some technologies go well beyond these examples by including the ability to infer new facts based on existing information.

Part 2 of this book provides an overview of semantic technologies and suggests how they may filter into our traditional tools to make the task of finding what we need easier.

5

Natural language processing

Although the study of how language works began in Ancient India and Ancient Greece, the modern field of linguistics dates back to the late 18th century. At that time it was discovered that languages with corresponding sounds and meanings had grown out of a common ancestor; this discovery was tracked throughout the 19th century. In the 20th century, scholars turned their attention to structural linguistics examining the internal structure of words and sentences (Newmeyer, 2008).

Language structure is typically defined by a grammar, a set of rules by which language is organized into units. The grammar guides *syntactic analysis*, which identifies individual words and breaks language into sentences and phrases. *Semantic analysis* seeks to identify the meaning of the words and phrases. Syntactic and semantic analysis techniques have been altered and refined over the years to give machines the ability to make sense of human language. These techniques are used for computer language processing, text processing, voice recognition, robot control, and other man-machine communications. Though natural language processing in this book has been introduced in the context of semantic search, it plays a role in many semantic technologies such as data mining systems, named entity extraction processes, and indexing and translation software.

Natural language processing or parsing (NLP) is the electronic processing of language. It was first considered by Alan Turing in 1950 when he asked 'Can machines think?' Turing proposed that if a person received responses to questions from a computer and from another person, and could not tell the person from the computer, then computers could indeed think (Turing, 1950). Although this conclusion could be argued, it constitutes the first suggestion that a computer should be able to understand natural language rather than forcing the user to accommodate to the machine at all times. The first natural language processing program, ELIZA, appeared in 1966. Using syntactic analysis, keywords, and rules, ELIZA emulates a therapist, demonstrating that computers can be programmed to understand natural language. (Try the web-enabled version at *http://www-ai .ijs.si/eliza/eliza.html.*)

NLP allows for the analysis of natural language so that its meaning may be recognized. A natural language parser typically breaks the sentence into smaller units and identifies the parts of speech, setting the stage for semantic analysis. Two different approaches are employed in syntactic analysis. One approach relies on defining the structure of language and determines meaning through the use of parts of speech or other appropriate labels, which entails the definition of a grammar. Historically, grammar-based approaches have completely parsed text to form a detailed structure modeling the text, which is a time-consuming process.

The other approach uses pattern matching and statistical analysis, which is significantly faster than defining the structure of language. Many voice recognition applications of today use these techniques. For example, the voice activated phone menu choices used by many businesses utilize statistical methods to 'understand' voice responses.

The current trend, however, is toward blending the use of grammars and statistics to provide better performance and accuracy. In every case, identifying parts of speech plays a critical role in completing the syntactic analysis. This chapter will begin by explaining the important task of part-of-speech (POS) tagging and then describe the difference between the grammatical and statistical approaches to parsing the sentence. Gaining a basic understanding of NLP will help in understanding how semantic technologies work.

Tagging parts of speech

Identifying parts of speech is an important step in laying the foundation for semantic analysis. Whether a grammar-based or statistical approach is used for syntactic analysis, statistics usually drive the tagging of the parts of speech of a sentence.

The Brown Corpus, created at Brown University in 1961, consists of 500 samples of English prose, carefully selected to be current (as of 1961) and representative of published material. W. N. Francis and H. Kucera published the Corpus along with statistical observations on the use of words. 'The purpose of the tagged corpus is to facilitate automatic or semi-automatic syntactic analysis' (Francis and Kucera, 1979). The most noteworthy contribution was the tagged version of the Corpus completed in 1979, which identifies the part of speech for every word in the Corpus and provides statistics that are useful in syntactic analysis.

Other standard corpora, such as the Lancaster–Oslo/Bergen Corpus (LOB) (Johansson, Leech, and Goodluck, 1978) and the Penn Treebank (University of Pennsylvania, 1999), have followed. Despite being dated and relatively small, the Brown

Corpus is still often used as a training set or to measure the effectiveness of part-of-speech taggers because it has been so thoroughly analyzed (Bender, 2001; Sampson, 2008; W3-Corpora Project, 1998; Yi, 2007).

Different POS tagging techniques provide varying levels of accuracy. Eugene Charniak suggests that a very simple algorithm will achieve 90% accuracy in assigning parts of speech if a corpus is used for its word frequencies. The algorithm assigns the most frequently used tag for each word that appears in the corpus and the tag *proper noun* to all unknown words (Charniak, 1997). This algorithm works fairly well because most words have an unambiguous part of speech; for example the words 'argument' and 'antonym' are always nouns. However, some words can be assigned different parts of speech depending on context. For example, the word 'can' is used both as a verb and as a noun:

> 'I can attend on the 15th.'
> 'The can rolled into the street.'

The POS tag is *ambiguous*; this is a common issue with natural language processing and various *disambiguation techniques* are used to address the issue. Statistics from a corpus may be used to disambiguate among tags. For example, the word 'can' appears 1,772 times in the Brown Corpus, most frequently as a verb, but also as a noun. The simple algorithm described above would always assign the verb tag to the word can because it is used more frequently that way. However, this simple disambiguation rule could improve POS tagging accuracy:

'When preceded by an article ("the can", "a can") "can" is tagged as a noun.' Otherwise, the basic rule applies and the verb tag is applied.

Grammar-based NLP

Natural language processing requires more than simply accurate POS tagging; it also requires the ability to group phrases. A symbolic grammar for a language defines the rules for how parts of speech are put together to convey meaning.

A very simple grammar might define a sentence as: a noun phrase followed by a verb followed by a noun phrase. For example, see the simple grammar defined in Table 5.1.

According to this grammar, the sentence 'Mary organized the bookshelf' could be parsed into the parse tree illustrated in Figure 5.1.

This is an example of a *deep* or full parsing where every word in the sentence is identified as a part of the grammar. Note that this simple grammar only allows for a very small number of parts of speech and very simple sentences; it would not be capable of parsing 'Mary gave the book to John' or 'Mary organized the messy bookshelf'. Defining a grammar suitable for deep parsing a natural language is a significant undertaking; the resulting grammar would be lengthy and complicated in order to understand complex sentences or sentences of significant length. It is precisely this concern that became an issue with voice recognition.

Table 5.1 **Definitions for parsing noun phrases in simple grammar**

Symbol	Meaning
S => NP V NP	A sentence consists of a noun phrase followed by a verb followed by another noun phrase.
NP => N | DT N	A noun phrase is made up of either a noun or a determinant followed by a noun.
DT => 'a' | 'the'	A determinant is either the word 'a' or the word 'the'.

Figure 5.1 Parse tree for 'Mary organized the bookshelf'

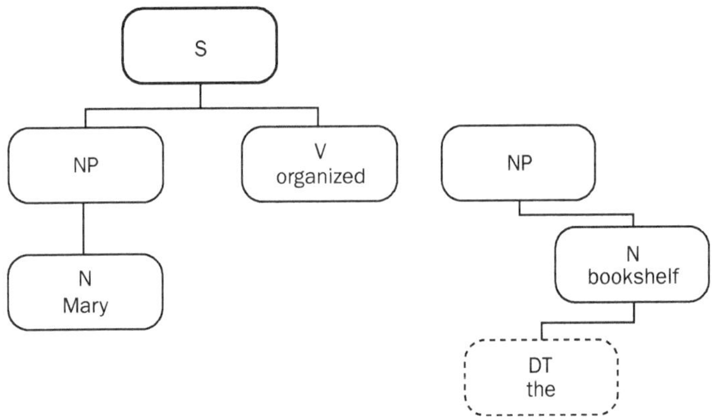

If a deep parsing method and complete grammar are used, it is not possible to analyze a spoken sentence rapidly enough to provide feedback to impatient human beings. Although the time required for processing text using deep parsing techniques is also slow, it was the performance requirements for voice recognition that fostered additional research into other approaches.

One approach to providing better performance is *partial* or *shallow parsing*, which consists of extracting key parts of speech in chunks. Partial parsing often provides sufficient detail to support analysis of meaning within a more reasonable time frame. A partial parsing of the first sentence of the Gettysburg address is shown in Figure 5.2. This partial parsing ignores prepositions and prepositional phrases. Although it misses an important point, that *all* men are created equal, the general sense of the statement is clear.

The creation of a grammar for any natural language is a significant task; a complete grammar for a natural language must define all possible correct grammatical expressions. Grammar-based systems are typically implemented using rules, each of which corresponds to a correct grammatical

Figure 5.2 **Partial parsing of the first sentence of the Gettysburg Address**

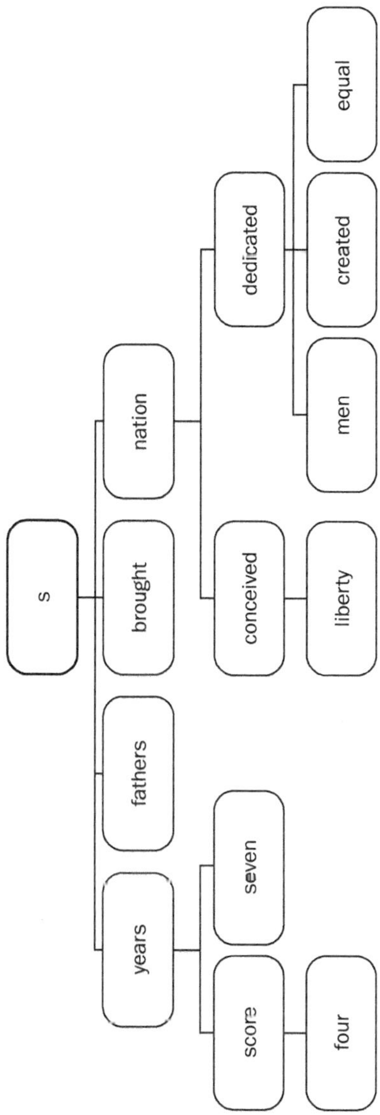

sentence or phrase. Parsing a sentence consists of executing or *firing* the collection of rules necessary to generate the sentence. Sentences are compared against thousands of rules to find the best possible match. The output, which theoretically resembles the tree structure displayed for the Gettysburg address, is typically output as tagged text that can be somewhat cryptic. For example, the following is the output of the CASS parser (Abney, 2006). This expression represents the phrase 'our fathers brought forth on this continent':

```
[nx
[prps our]
[nns fathers]]
[vnp
[vnx
[vbn brought]]
[rb forth]
[pp
[in on]
[nx
[dtp this]
[nn continent]]]]
[',',]
```

Although grammar-based NLP is a proven technique, performance remains an issue. Statistical methods are providing performance improvements that make semantic technologies more feasible and reliable.

Statistical NLP

In addition to the statistical methods used in part-of-speech tagging, statistical or probabilistic methods can provide a better performing alternative to the grammar-based systems just described. Rather than developing a full grammar for the language, statistical information derived from a *training set*, or corpus, is used to determine syntactic structure. This approach depends heavily on large amounts of data that are representative of the natural language. One can imagine that this method might be error-prone, but with a carefully selected training set, the results can be surprisingly accurate.

In the most basic statistical technique, a complete grammar is provided by a linguist and rule-based parsing is performed to gather statistics on how frequently each rule is used in parsing the training set. The rules are then ordered by frequency. When new text is parsed, the system fires rules in the order of frequency, stopping when it finds an acceptable parse of a sentence. For example, we might have the probabilities for parsing noun phrases based on a corpus shown in Table 5.2.

Therefore when the parser encounters a noun phrase, it would first attempt to parse the entire sentence assuming that the noun phrase is parsed by grammar rule 3, which has the highest probability. If this leads to a failure – a point at which the parser cannot continue to parse the sentence – then the parser retraces its steps and tries the next most probable grammar rule for the noun phrase.

Other approaches *learn* the grammar *from* the training set, defining rules as it processes text, rather than having the rules spelled out in the beginning. The difference, however, is that it is possible that this parsing method may fail to process some sentences because no sequence of rules can be found to produce the sentence. This is because the grammar is learned and some grammatical structures that are perfectly acceptable simply may not appear in the training set. For example, perhaps the corpus did not contain any example of

Table 5.2 **Probabilities for parsing noun phrases in statistical grammar**

Rule	Symbol	Meaning	Example	Probability
1	NP => DT N N	A noun phrase consists of a determinant followed by a noun followed by another noun.	the apple pie	.15
2	NP => N	A noun phrase is made up of a noun.	Mary	.3
3	NP => DT N	A noun phrase is made up of a determinant followed by a noun.	the bookshelf	.5
4	NP => NP NP	A noun phrase consists of a noun phrase followed by another noun phrase.	20 dollars per person	.05

a noun phrase followed by phrase (Rule 4 in Table 5.2). Then the resulting grammar would not be able to parse 'twenty dollars a person'. This seems an imperfect approach.

Partial parsing techniques for statistical NLP are often based on a lexical model that identifies the most important word in a phrase, the *head* of the phrase. The lexical model defines a set of rules by which sentences may be reduced to smaller units. Using a training set, statistics may be compiled based on the frequency of the lexical rules. Using the same technique of executing rules according to the frequency of their appearance in the training set, the combination of partial parsing and statistics allows the material to be parsed more rapidly.

Semantic analysis

Regardless of whether the syntactic analysis technique is grammar-based or statistics-based, at the conclusion of the parsing and POS tagging, a symbolic representation of the sentence is produced. Previously considered the domain of NLP, semantic analysis is now often where natural language processing leaves off and semantic tools begin. In order to make sense of the symbolic representation, that is, to find what you are looking for, you must specify some criteria or means by which to identify material of interest. Most search engines simply use a pattern matching technique to match the keywords you enter in the search window. Using semantic analysis, it is possible to specify what you are looking for in a more meaningful way. Semantic technologies add value by simplifying the task of defining the criteria, matching the criteria *semantically* to a set of documents, and then returning the results in a user-friendly manner. Approaches for matching criteria semantically are discussed further in later chapters.

Current applications of NLP

Fortunately, search engines and other knowledge management tools typically incorporate NLP into their systems eliminating the need for your average user to evaluate and select natural language processing tools. For example, Nervana's semantic search and knowledge discovery tools are based on NLP, as is Linguamatics I2E. CognitionSearch employs linguistics and mathematical algorithms. Language Weaver and Google are using statistical analysis of language to provide translations from one natural language to another. An ontology-based approach to language translation would identify the concepts represented in the document and then use grammar rules to construct the same sentence in a different natural language. A statistical approach would use a training set of translated text to pair sentence structure and words between the two languages.

Key concepts

- A natural language *parser* typically breaks the sentence into smaller units and identifies the parts of speech, setting the stage for semantic analysis.
- A *part-of-speech (POS) tagger* plays an important role in laying the foundation for semantic analysis. POS tagging is based on the statistical analysis of a body of documents, a *corpus*. *Sentence diagrams* are a good model to understand POS tagging. Some words may take on different POS tags in different contexts; *disambiguation techniques* are required.
- Parsers are based on either:
  - a *grammar*, which defines the language structure, identifies individual words, and breaks the language into sentences and phrases, or
  - *pattern matching and statistical analysis*, which improves the accuracy and performance of NLP.
- *Deep parsing* is a technique that requires that every word be assigned a POS tag.
- *Shallow or partial parsing* extracts key parts of a sentence in chunk and assigns POS tags to the entire chunk.

6

Using metadata to add semantic information

Semantic technologies require the ability to understand the meaning of natural language. *Annotating* the document with information about its meaning is another approach to adding semantics. Metadata, or information about data, has been used for decades. Historically, it has been stored in separate files or in relational databases. For example, citations consist of information about a source and are often stored in a card catalog or its electronic equivalent. Embedding metadata within documents gave birth to a family of structured languages, from the Standard General Markup Language (SGML) to the eXtensible Markup Language (XML) to the Resource Description Framework (RDF). They are described briefly in the first section below and the most commonly used structured languages, XML and RDF, receive a more in-depth treatment in Chapter 12. The mechanism for embedding metadata within documents using structured languages is called metadata tagging or simply *tagging*; it is described in the last two sections of this chapter.

Structured languages

The earliest standard markup language, the Standard General Markup Language (SGML), was first developed in

1970, based on work done at IBM, and was accepted as a standard by the International Standards Organization (ISO) in 1986. SGML is actually a meta-language – a language that defines other languages, specifically markup languages. Markup languages support marking up documents or tagging them with metadata. However, embedding metadata requires a specific vocabulary which defines the acceptable metadata fields (Gaynor, 1996; Goldfarb, 1997). The controlled vocabulary, or the set of tag names that are permitted, is defined at the start of the SGML document. This flexibility allows different software to interpret tags differently. However, it also leaves the interpretation of the vocabulary up to the reader of the document and makes generic processing a challenge, especially for the large volumes of data on the web.

SGML was the basis for the Library of Congress MAchine Readable Cataloging Document (MARC) record (Library of Congress, 2007), which is the electronic form of a card from a card catalog.

XML has largely supplanted SGML; it is a subset of SGML that enforces restrictions intended to facilitate managing resources on the web. For example, external references must contain a system identifier; this enables XML documents to faithfully locate references anywhere on the web. End tags are required for all tags, which makes parsing the XML document easier and more reliable. This is a simple example of an XML citation:

```
<?xml version="1.0"?>
<book>
  <title>With Malice Toward None</title>
  <subtitle>A Life of Abraham Lincoln</subtitle>
  <author>Stephen B. Oates</author>
  <chapter title="Rivers of Time">
```

```
    <para>Outside of Illinois, people knew little about
him. Even newspapers were ....</para>
      ...
  </chapter>
...
</book> (Oates, 1994)
```

Bibliographic software such as EndNote and RefWorks are often able to export records tagged with XML. This metadata is typically not embedded within the text itself, but is encoded within the fields so that it can be easily exported. Here is an excerpt from PubMed's XML export of an article:

```
<PubmedArticle>
 <MedlineCitation Owner='NLM' Status='MEDLINE'>
 <PMID>16937748</PMID>
  <Article PubModel='Print'>
  <Journal>
  <ISSN IssnType='Print'>1081-1206</ISSN>
  <JournalIssue CitedMedium='Print'>
  <Volume>97</Volume>
  <Issue>2</Issue>
  <PubDate>
   <Year>2006</Year>
   <Month>Aug</Month>
  </PubDate>
  </JournalIssue>
  <Title>Annals of allergy, asthma &amp;
immunology: official publication of the American
College of Allergy, Asthma, &amp;
Immunology</Title>
  <ISOAbbreviation>Ann. Allergy Asthma Immunol.
  </ISOAbbreviation>
```

</Journal>
<ArticleTitle>Assessment of adrenal suppression in children with asthma treated with inhaled corticosteroids: use of dehydroepiandrosterone sulfate as a screening test. </ArticleTitle>
<Pagination>
<MedlinePgn>182-6</MedlinePgn>
</Pagination>
<AuthorList CompleteYN=‘Y’>
<Author ValidYN=‘Y’>
<LastName>Dorsey</LastName>
<ForeName>Morna J</ForeName>
</Author>
<Author ValidYN=‘Y’>
<LastName>Cohen</LastName>
<ForeName>Laurie E</ForeName>
</Author>
<Author ValidYN=‘Y’>
<LastName>Phipatanakul</LastName>
<ForeName>Wanda</ForeName>
</Author>
<Author ValidYN=‘Y’>
<LastName>Denufrio</LastName>
<ForeName>Danielle</ForeName>
</Author>
<Author ValidYN=‘Y’>
<LastName>Schneider</LastName>
<ForeName>Lynda C</ForeName>
</Author>
</AuthorList>
</Article>
</PubmedData>
</PubmedArticle> (Dorsey et al., 2006)

Two of the concerns about XML are that the tags are defined in a Document Type Definition (DTD) (a language different from XML) and that XML is unable to capture meaning. The RDF addresses these issues by supporting several built-in rules about hierarchical relationships and extends hierarchy rules to relationships as well as to concepts. RDF is more fully described in Chapter 12.

The examples above demonstrate the use of structured languages for storing metadata separately from the data it describes. This presents problems of connecting the correct metadata with its subject and separates information about meaning from the document itself.

Metadata tagging

Tagging involves adding metadata *within* the document. A number of specific tagging standards are available for different domains; two of the most often cited tagging standards are the Text Encoding Initiative and the Dublin Core Metadata Initiative.

The Text Encoding Initiative (TEI; *http://www.tei-c.org*) is dedicated to developing standards for representing documents in digital form. Its website provides an example of embedded metadata (see *http://www.tei-c.org/Guidelines/Customization/Lite/U5-anal.html*). This is taken from Chapter 38 of *Jane Eyre*:

> READER, I married him. A quiet wedding we had: he and I, the parson and clerk, were alone present. When we got back from church, I went into the kitchen of the manor-house, where Mary was cooking the dinner, and John cleaning the knives, and I said – 'Mary, I have been married to Mr Rochester this morning.' The housekeeper and her husband were of that decent, phlegmatic order

of people, to whom one may at any time safely communicate a remarkable piece of news without incurring the danger of having one's ears pierced by some shrill ejaculation and subsequently stunned by a torrent of wordy wonderment. Mary did look up, and she did stare at me; the ladle with which she was basting a pair of chickens roasting at the fire, did for some three minutes hang suspended in air, and for the same space of time John's knives also had rest from the polishing process; but Mary, bending again over the roast, said only – 'Have you, miss? Well, for sure!'

Using TEI guidelines (Burnard and Sperberg-McQueen, 2006) to define the structure, that is the chapter (div type), paragraph (p), sentences (s), and page breaks (pb), of the text we have:

```
<pb n="474"/>
<div type="chapter" n="38">
<p><s n="001">Reader, I married him.</s>
<s n="002">A quiet wedding we had:</s>
<s n="003">he and I, the parson and clerk, were
alone present.</s>
<s n="004">When we got back from church, I went into
the kitchen of the manor-house, where Mary was cooking
the dinner, and John cleaning the knives, and I said —</s>
</p>
<p>
<q>
<s n="005">Mary, I have been married to
Mr Rochester this morning.</s>
</q>
...
</p>
</div>
```

Note that this particular set of tags helps us to understand the structure of the text but not the meaning.

One of the disadvantages of embedded tagging is clear in even this simple example: it is harder for people to read. Various XML editing programs can provide a structured view of the document using the tags as a guide, which is easier to read, but they can still be awkward with large collections of text.

Specialized editors can facilitate the task further. For example, the Digital Collection System (DCS) is an application provided by the Digital Library for Earth Science Education. Contributors use the DCS application to describe research materials, web-based educational resources, terms and definitions, career news, earth data sets, and more according to several metadata standards, including ADEPT/DLESE/NASA and the Dublin Core. But more generally and importantly, DCS supports any metadata standards defined in XML.

Semantic tagging

Typically, metadata is defined very generally as data about data; it does not help us to understand the meaning of the text. However, by tagging based on knowledge structures such as thesauri, subject headings or taxonomy categories, semantic information can be embedded.

The Dublin Core initiative was launched in 1995 by the Online Computer Library Center (OCLC) to 'facilitate the finding, sharing and management of information' (Dublin Core Metadata Initiative, 2007). It identifies 15 elements including Title, Creator, Subject, Description, Publisher, and so on, each of which has attributes of name, label, URI definition, type of term and may have optional attributes including references, member of, broader than, narrower than, has range, and so on. Through the use of its hierarchical relationships – broader than, narrower than – and other relationships such as has range, has domain, and member of, the Dublin Core captures semantics.

Scorpion, a research project of the OCLC, is open source software that automates the classification of text documents on the web using a subject classification scheme or thesaurus. The subject headings or thesaurus that must be translated into a Scorpion database is created from an SGML file which defines concepts as illustrated in the following example:

```
<rec>
 <ScorpionCaption>Robots</ScorpionCaption>
 <ScorpionNum>629.892</ScorpionNum>
 <ScorpionKeywords>robotics, evolutionary robotics,
parallel robots</ScorpionKeywords>
 <ScorpionTerms>industrial robots;
robotics</ScorpionTerms>
 <ScorpionHierarchy>Technology (Applied sciences);
Engineering and allied operations; (Other branches of
engineering); Computer Control</ScorpionHierarchy>
</rec>
```

Creating a Scorpion database for your own subject heading or thesaurus requires a little software programming, but the project makes the Dewey Decimal Classification and Library of Congress systems available. The Scorpion software then processes a document according to the database and creates an annotated version.

Another example of semantic annotation is the KIM Platform from Ontotext (Ontotext, 2008). This platform stores semantic metadata separately from the document itself. Figure 6.1 depicts the relationship between the actual document and the markup that leads to related information in a sort of semantic network.

KIM annotates named entities (people, organizations, locations) and key phrases, which are groups of words frequently found strung together in the documents submitted. Statistical pattern matching determines which key phrases will be annotated. These are called *semantic features* of the document. KIM is an ontology-based annotation tool; it has an ontology with over 200,000 concepts defined. A graphical user interface which runs on either Windows or Linux allows the user to add documents to a storage location. As documents are added to this location, named entities and key phrases are pulled out and added to the ontology. Then the documents

Figure 6.1 **KIM Platform: the relationship between a document and markup**

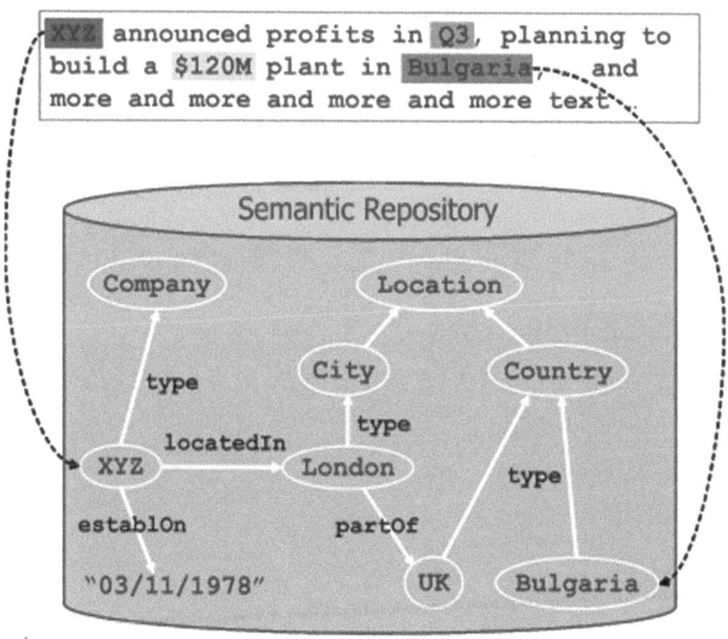

Source: *http://www.ontotext.com/kim/semanticannotation.html*

themselves are annotated with hyperlinks to the ontology. KIM also provides a programming interface that allows users to develop customized applications that implement semantic queries, named entity search, and exploration of the ontology.

Key concepts

- *Metadata*, defined simply as data about data, has been used for decades to describe documents more fully. Metadata can also be used to add semantic dimensions to documents.
- *Markup languages* such as Standard General Markup Language (SGML), eXtensible Markup Language (XML), and Resource Description Framework (RDF) can be used to write metadata that describes documents.
- *Tagging* is the process of embedding metadata within the documents themselves. Dublin Core is a type of tagging developed by OCLC and well known in the field of library science.

7

Other semantic capabilities

Semantic capabilities can be used for purposes other than natural language search. Having the meaning of a document represented, rather than just the text, is useful in a variety of situations. This chapter will cover how simply classifying a document within a knowledge structure can give it meaning, how topic maps can be created to show properties other than hierarchical placement, and how the semantic capabilities of rules engines are used for the creation of decision support mechanisms.

Semantic classification

For librarians, the concept of classification may be a familiar area of providing semantic information about a document. Classification provides semantic information by virtue of the fact that a subject matter expert has selected the category that has most meaning for this document. Some classification schemes are simply a list of headings or categories; others add meaning of their own. Taxonomies, for example, provide relationships such as broader than or narrower than to indicate whether a particular category is a subset or a superset of another.

While the Dewey Decimal System allows for material to be found in one (and only one) place, classification schemes allow for subject headings to be associated with material so that it can be found using more than one avenue. For example, the Medical Subjects Heading classification scheme (MeSH) from the National Library of Medicine (NLM) is used to classify medical citations for the PubMed database. MeSH provides at least three different ways to arrive at documents about 'AIDS related opportunistic infections':

Bacterial Infections and Mycoses [C01]
    Infection [C01.539]
        Opportunistic Infections [C01.539.597]
            AIDS_Related Opportunistic Infections [C01.539.597.050]

Immune System Diseases [C20]
    Immunologic Deficiency Syndromes [C20.673]
        HIV Infections [C20.673.480]
            AIDS-Related Opportunistic Infections [C20.673.480.100]

Virus Diseases [C02]
    RNA Virus Infections [C02.782]
        Retroviridae Infections [C02.782.815]
            Lentivirus Infections [C02.782.815.616]
                HIV Infections [C02.782.815.616.400]
                    AIDS-Related Opportunistic Infections [C02.782.815.616 .400.100]

Within PubMed, by entering the MeSH term in the search window, all documents tagged with this MeSH term are returned as results. The classification of citations according to MeSH terms is performed by subject matter experts at the NLM and other selected organizations.

Semantic classification can be provided by referencing any number of semantic knowledge structures from thesauri and taxonomies to synonym sets (*synsets*), topic maps, and ontologies.

Synsets

Synonym sets convey meaning by relating groups of terms as synonyms. The term synset was essentially defined by WordNet, an effort that began in 1985 at Princeton University and aimed to provide a browser-friendly way of navigating through words related by meaningful connections.

A synset can be used to expand queries to databases. For example, rather than entering just the word 'cancer' into a database, a user who consults WordNet first may also choose to add 'OR malignant neoplastic disease' to the query. This would enable a text-based search engine to find a broader range of information.

Google Labs provides a feature called Google Sets, which allows users to submit a few terms in a set and Google returns more items from that set. The example provided on their homepage appears clear enough: when you enter *bmw*, *honda*, and *mercedes benz*, the set Google returns contains named of other automobile companies. The relationship among the terms Google returns is not made explicit, which may not be as useful. For example, if a user enters *koala*, *kangaroo*, and *wombat* hoping to find a list of other marsupials, she may be disappointed to see that Google's set includes many other animals found in Australia, but they are not necessarily all marsupials. Google provides no guidance on how this feature might be incorporated in the future to provide better searching capabilities, but the tool could be a useful way to find related items within a certain category.

Synsets may be used manually by users to search or to embed markup such as keywords or classification categories to documents. Automated use of WordNet's synsets is found in tools that provide query expansion (used in federated search), documentation classification, information retrieval (search), and automated translation (Morato et al., 2004).

Topic maps

Topic maps are another way to create structured information about documents that can be electronically processed. Topic maps are a subject-based classification technique that provide a rich classification mechanism and can support more precise search and navigation. They are guided by an International Standards Organization (ISO) standard (ISO, 1999).

Topic maps have topics (concepts), associations (relationships), and occurrences (metadata about a topic) (TopicMaps.Org Authoring Group, 2001). One topic may have any number of names and different topics may have the same name. Topics also have a type, for example *Hamlet* and *Romeo and Juliet* are types of plays. Associations might connect the titles of these plays with the characters in them, such as Hamlet, Ophelia, Romeo, Juliet, and Benvolio. Occurrences might include the author of the plays or the years in which they were each written.

Topic maps differ from taxonomies and most classification schemes because they create a network of related topics rather than providing a hierarchical organization, but relationships are defined more specifically. For example, the topic map shown in Figure 7.1 is a representation of the relationships between SGML, XML, topic maps, various query languages, and so on. It provides a detailed perspective of the relationships – more detailed and specific than we would be

Figure 7.1 **Topic map showing the relationship between SGML, XML, topic maps, and various query languages**

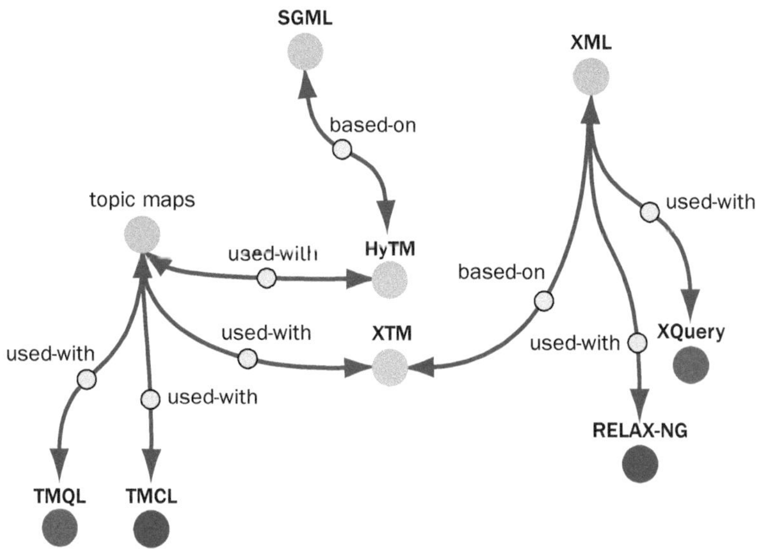

Source: *http://www.hipertexto.info/images/topicmap.gif*

able to express in a taxonomy or other classification scheme without adding a great deal of complexity. Topic maps are defined in a structured language, XML.

Topic types:

- SGML, XML, and topic maps are technologies.
- TMQL and XQuery are query languages.
- TMCL and RELAX-NG are constraint languages.
- HyTM and XTM are interchange formats.

Associations:

- Topic maps are 'used-with' XTM, HyTM, TMCL, and TMQL.
- XTM is 'based on' XML.

Rules and inference

Rules engines are another important semantic technology; they are specialized software tools for processing rules efficiently. Rules provide the ability to infer new facts or *assertions* from an initial set of facts, the *factbase*. Rules can be expressed simply as 'if–then' statements where the 'if' part of the statement is called the *antecedent* and the 'then' part is called the *consequent*:

> If a person uses semantic technology, then the person is using state-of-the-art techniques.
>
> If a person uses state-of-the-art techniques, then the person is efficient.
>
> If a person is efficient, then the person is well paid.

If we know that Jane is a person and that she uses semantic technology, then we can infer the following facts about Jane:

> Jane is efficient.
>
> Jane is well paid.

This seemingly simple technique of firing rules that lead to new inferences makes rules engines powerful tools, but when the rules number in the hundreds of thousands, processing can be very time-consuming. Two different methods are used to implement rules engines. *Forward chaining rules engines* start with a fact and find a rule whose antecedent matches and then continues to fire rules in this way until all possible rules have been fired. *Backward chaining engines* begin with a consequent and try to confirm whether it is true or not, based on the facts already known.

Thus, the process begins by finding a consequent that matches and then uses the antecedent of this rule to find all antecedents that can be assumed to be true for this fact; the process continues until there are no more rules to match. There are appropriate uses for both techniques. If most rules have more antecedents than consequents, then forward chaining is preferred because matching all the conditions will be difficult and thus will lead to fewer rule firings – less work to do to reach the end of the process. If rules have more consequents than antecedents then, following the same logic, a backward chaining rules engine would be more efficient.

The process of selecting which rules to fire and in which order to fire them presents challenges of its own. In the case of a forward chaining engine, the rules could be fired in a specific order; as soon as a match is found, firing stops for that antecedent, thus abandoning the remaining rules. There are several methods for ordering the rules. Rules could be fired according to the order in which they were added to the factbase, or perhaps the rules are ordered according to some other criteria. Regardless of the ordering method, the algorithm selects the first rule that matches the antecedent and fires it abandoning matching additional rules. A second method depends on maintaining statistics about how frequently a rule is fired; this is essentially imposing an order on the rule and selecting the first, the most frequently fired, rule. The most specific rule could be fired, that is, fire the rule with the largest number of antecedents that can be matched with currently known facts. The task of building a rules engine is beginning to sound more difficult.

Many existing industry decision support systems are essentially rule-based. But since the business rules are often built into the software, the systems are difficult to change as rules change. The following car insurance example provides a case in point.

Antecedent:

- The car is red.
- The car is in a sport class.
- The driver is male.
- The driver is between the ages of 16 and 25.

Consequent:

- The insurance premium is increased by 20%. (Wiseman, 2006)

Perhaps new statistics show that females in the same age range have the same number of claims as males or perhaps that the age range should be extended to 27 years of age. The insurance company can only remain a viable business as long as it can keep up with current statistics and adjust rates accordingly. Instead of just changing the wording of the rules, the company now needs to change the software itself.

Key concepts

- *Semantic classification* can be provided by referencing any number of semantic knowledge structures from thesauri and taxonomies to synonym sets (*synsets*), topic maps, and ontologies.
- A *synset* is a group of words with synonymous connections and can be used to expand queries or aid with documentation classification.

- *Topic maps* consist of topics (concepts), associations (relationships), and occurrences (metadata about a topic). They are different from most classification schemes because they create a network of related topics rather than providing a hierarchical organization.
- *Rules engines* provide the ability to *infer* new facts from a *factbase*, making them a powerful semantic tool. Rules are essentially 'if–then' statements where the 'if' part of the statement is called the *antecedent*; the 'then' part is called the *consequent*.

Part 3
Case studies: theory into practice

Part 1 introduced the concept of an ontology, described how to create one and explained how semantic search can be implemented using an ontology. Part 2 described a number of other semantic technologies that provide the foundations for current and future semantic applications. Now that you have an understanding of how ontologies and semantics work in theory, you can see how these technologies are helping to establish real-world solutions for current problems in a variety of industries.

Each chapter in Part 3 presents a description of a problem in an organization, explores how that organization uses ontologies and semantic technologies as part of a solution, and offers insight into what these groups will do next to continue improving their technology into the future.

8

Biogen Idec: using semantics in drug discovery research

The cost of developing a new medication is reported by the Tufts Center for the Study of Drug Discovery to be approximately $800 million per new drug (DiMasi, Hansen, and Grabowski, 2003). Although some industry critics put the cost at $100 million per new discovery (Angell, 2005), with an investment of between $100 and $800 million dollars, it is no surprise that biotech and pharmaceutical companies conduct careful literature searches before investing in the development of a new drug or treatment. If existing patents limit the company's ability to move forward on a research problem, they need to know about it at the start. If they want to recruit experts in a disease, treatment, or therapeutic area, they will need to identify who is making strides in the literature. If they need to know what has most recently been published in a specific realm of research, they will need to find the most up-to-date information available. With all of these research needs, it is critical that information professionals are available as expert consultants to the staff.

For an information services group to be successful in this setting, there are four necessary components:

- a collection of data sources
- a collection of tools to search, organize, and deliver the relevant knowledge from those data sources

- a person with skills in searching and organization, i.e. a professional librarian
- a person with expert knowledge of the domain who can filter the data, make connections to other concepts that might be relevant, and increase the creativity and complexity of the query; i.e. a domain expert working within the information services group.

Biogen Idec, a biotechnology company specializing in oncology, neurology, and immunology treatments, has established all four of these components in their Library and Literature Informatics Department. When serving the 1,500 professional staff of Biogen Idec, the library research team is responsible for fulfilling a wide range of information requests. Through careful analysis of their reference queries, they have determined that 80% of the requests are seeking a specific answer (e.g. What is the clinical population of multiple sclerosis patients in India?). These queries require high precision, but low recall. The remaining 20% of the queries require a deliverable that can only be achieved by extensive literature analysis or text mining. These research projects may require an ongoing search with high recall and precision, or extracting specific information from a large number of documents (e.g. Retrieve all adverse events associated with cancer-related protein kinases) and correspondingly use a great deal more human resources than requests seeking a specific answer (Roberts and Hayes, 2008).

When a patron submits a research request, the Library and Literature Informatics Group must first determine what deliverable is required by the patron. Do they want a specific answer to a question (e.g. What drugs are prescribed for lupus?) or do they want all related papers that they can review on their own? Perhaps, an alert needs to be set up for a work group using a sophisticated query to improve recall and precision. Or the patron may need a custom database of specific information extracted from the literature and combined with selected structured databases. The type of deliverable determines how intensive their research project must be, which data sources they will draw from, and what tools will be used to present the results to the patron.

The Biogen Idec Library uses a variety of data sources, including Medline, Dialog, OMIM (Online Mendelian Inheritance in Man, a catalog of human genes and genetic disorders), full text Open Access literature, patent literature, biological sequence databases, and corpora derived using QUOSA information management software. The semi-structured sources, such as OMIM and Medline, have bibliographic metadata built into them. The team also conducts free text searches with semi-structured data sources such as collections of disease indicators and patent databases. They use more specialized tools such as Basic Local Alignment Search Tool (BLAST) (which finds regions of similarity between genetic sequences within specific areas of interest), EntrezGene (curated information about genes located in specific positions on the chromosomes), and Sage (which analyzes gene expression patterns).

Though having access to this vast quantity of tools is beneficial, learning how to use all of them well is a significant undertaking. Because each of the tools operates differently from the others, the burden is on users to learn the best techniques for acquiring the information they need. This requirement for special expertise for different tools and data resources fosters an environment where an information professional cannot possibly master all of the tools, so members of the research team each specialize in a few. The saying 'It takes a village' takes on new meaning since collaboration between multiple experts in the library is required for nearly any significant research project to ensure that project objectives are achieved (Davies, 2006).

A research request may result in the need to extract information from dozens to millions of documents to build the requested database. However, this analysis can take weeks to years using standard search and manual curation methods, and patrons are often unwilling to wait that long to move ahead on their projects. Often, the research project has a deadline which results in just a fraction of the answer being returned owing to time and resource restrictions. It is clear that a reduction in time and staff resources spent on identifying the requested information would greatly improve the research product by making it more comprehensive, precise, and cost-effective. How can semantic technologies help to solve this problem?

Biogen Idec's solution

Biogen Idec uses text analytics, the process of extracting structured information from unstructured text, to help make their work more efficient. This process of analyzing unstructured text is aided by ontologies. Text mining requires thesauri that include terms that may be found in the literature; formal taxonomies or controlled vocabularies such as MeSH and the Systemized Nomenclature of Medicine (SNOMED) were not designed for text mining and use terminology that describes the literature, but is not found within it. For example, a subject heading 'Bone marrow, transplanted' is unlikely to be found within unstructured text, but the less formal phrase 'transplanted bone marrow' is likely to be found. When ontologies and these thesauri are available in the text mining process, it is easier for information professionals to find and/or extract that for which they are looking.

The Library and Literature Informatics Department also relies heavily on two text mining tools that are relevant to semantic technologies. QUOSA retrieves full text articles and allows one to organize and share documents of interest. It is often used by the Library to develop specialized sub-corpora for further text analytics workflows. Linguamatics I2E uses a powerful natural language parser and semantic analysis to mine text and extract information (Davies, 2006).

QUOSA provides federated searching across multiple literature sources such as Medline, OVID, Scopus, Web of Knowledge, full text indices provided by journal publishers, and even a company's internal documents. The full text of documents can be retrieved depending on journal licensing, and the user is able to run searches on this literature. This capability can be useful when seeking information that may only be found in the Methods and Results section of a journal article.

The Linguamatics I2E product that Biogen Idec uses is a semantic search and text-mining tool. The program employs knowledge sources such as thesauri, taxonomies, and ontologies to semantically tag the literature and expand the user's query to include synonyms and other ways to represent a conceptual class (disease, protein, chemical compound, etc.), resulting in better recall and thus more comprehensive results. Syntactic restrictions can be combined with semantic classes to yield more precise information extraction. For example, a searcher can specify that the names of tissues be extracted when nuclear hormone receptor proteins are known to be expressed. This can be accomplished by searching for <semantic class: protein> <syntax: preposition> <syntax: noun phrase including the word 'tissue(s)'>. I2E is also capable of discovering connections *within* the text, based on part-of-speech tagging and other linguistic analysis techniques and syntactic proximity (e.g. within phrase, sentence, paragraph, section, document). I2E can search for facts and relationships within a corpus developed from QUOSA search results, thus combining the strengths of two text-mining tools to create a rich semantically typed dataset. The database of extracted information may then be imported into a workflow management tool, such as Inforsense. Inforsense can be used to mine the data within the structured information. In fact, the phrase 'text/data mining' is often used to describe the process of creating structured data from unstructured text.

The Library and Literature Informatics department has also taken advantage of semantically typed metadata, for example authors and institutions, to find experts in a specific scientific field. A tool called Cytoscape can display graphics showing connections among co-authors and associated universities or companies. This visual representation of domain experts in a specific area can be a very useful tool in identifying universities, companies, research labs or authors who are essentially hubs of activity.

The semantic tools and text analytics applications used by Biogen Idec combine to provide a powerful text-mining and search strategy, enabling its Library and Literature Informatics Department to sift efficiently through all available text and data resources using advanced query and information extraction technology to find the most relevant and comprehensive information currently possible.

The future

One direction for Biogen Idec's immediate future is to meet the need for better competitive intelligence by incorporating information from news services into the workflows developed for research. The same processes described above for collecting, parsing, filtering and deploying this information would be applied to this task, providing business development and product marketing teams with more sophisticated up-to-the-minute and precise information about competitive and collaborative drugs, treatments, and business ventures. Biogen Idec is currently developing the capability to extract semantically typed information from relevant news feeds using Linguamatics I2E and to deliver it to patrons for follow-up analysis.

While the Library and Literature Informatics Department has developed various internal synonym lists for use with text mining, they believe that engaging in pre-competitive collaboration with other biotechnology experts would yield more comprehensive thesauri. Although ontologies are being developed commercially and in the public domain, they are currently incomplete and generally difficult to modify. The team believes that with the amount of information available, the only way to ensure that the available and extensive literature resources can be effectively utilized is to work collaboratively to develop and share open-source tools and resources across the bioPharma industry.

9

The Center on Media and Child Health: using an ontology to explore the effects of media

Today, the average American child between the ages of eight and 18 spends six hours and 21 minutes a day with media (Roberts, Foehr, and Rideout, 2005), 18% of children aged zero to two have a television set in their bedrooms (Vandewater et al., 2007), and the video game industry reported sales of $18.55 billion in 2007 (Entertainment Software Association, 2008). Media are ubiquitous and have become a large part of our environment; people search the internet on their handheld wireless devices, advertisements seem to be omnipresent, and everyone on the subway has their own MP3 player. Many people wonder what effects these all-consuming technologies have on social, emotional, and physical health, especially that of children and adolescents.

Researchers have been examining the effects of media since the advent of radio, when parents wondered whether children would be adversely affected after listening to crime dramas. With the introduction of television in the 1950s, even more people became concerned about media, eventually leading to a massive research effort for the 1972 US Surgeon General's Report on the Impact of Televised Violence. In the 21st century, researchers are desperately trying to keep up with learning about the effects of an onslaught of new technologies that seem to appear every few months.

In 2003 the Center on Media and Child Health (CMCH) at Children's Hospital in Boston launched an ambitious effort to provide a database of research on the topic of media and their effects on the health of children and adolescents. This research came not only from fields like medicine and communications, but also from gender studies, psychology, and others. In addition to being able to gather all of this research together for the academic community, another important aim was to communicate scientific evidence about media effects to the general public. CMCH set out to create a free, online database that would:

- bring together existing research from all disciplines on the effects of media on child health
- be searchable by researchers, parents, teachers, and policymakers
- be accessible by novice users as well as expert searchers.

After gathering a large corpus of citations, the next task was to make this research broadly available. CMCH designed an interface for a Boolean search engine where users could choose between a variety of parameters, allowing them to make a free-text search or to specify subject headings, sources of funding, age groups, study designs, peer-reviewed status, or reference types (Figure 9.1).

Figure 9.1 **Screenshot of the CMCH Database of Research search page**

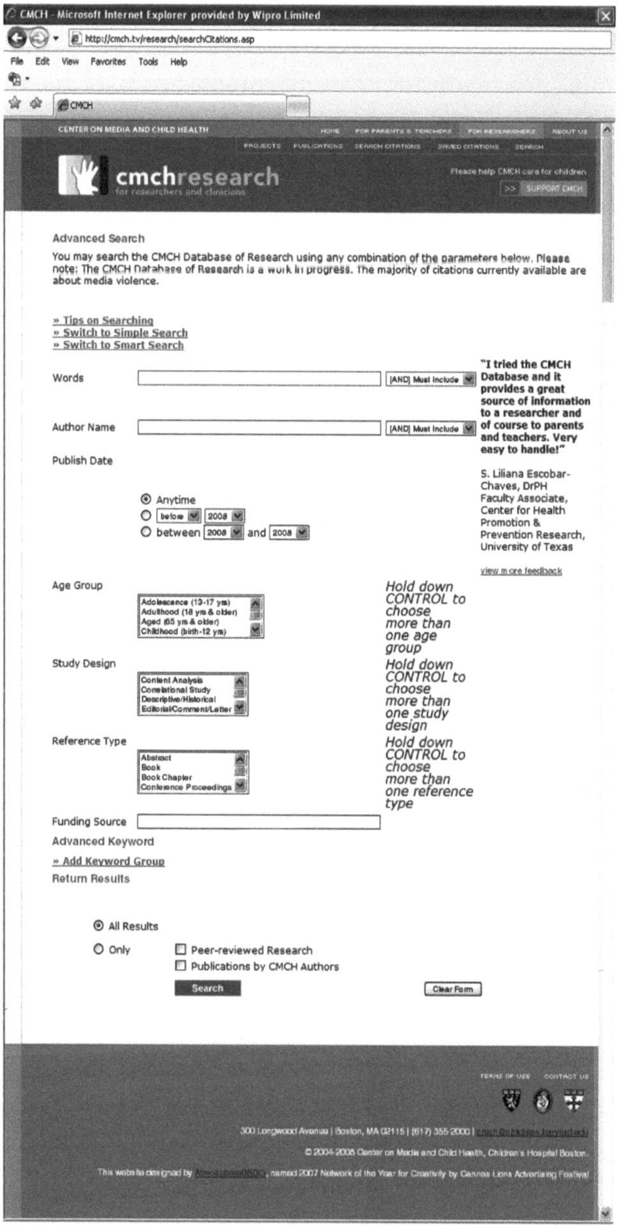

Source: *http://cmch.tv/research/searchCitations.asp*

Creating authority lists for most of these fields was straightforward; however, the issue of subject headings required more thought. The Dewey Decimal Classification and Library of Congress (LC) systems were examined to determine what subject headings might apply to the media. In Dewey:

- 000 Generalities
  - 028 – Reading, use of other information media
  - 070 – News media, journalism and publishing

In LC, some of the choices for media are:

- H – Social Sciences
  - HE – Transportation and Communications
    - HE8689-8700.95 – Radio and Television Broadcasting
- M – Music
  - ML – Literature on Music
    - ML3916-3918 – Social and Political Aspects of Music

It became clear that none of these classification systems would be specific enough to cover the effects of media at a level of detail that would distinguish the thousands of studies on media from each other. This meant that CMCH would need to create its own authority list. Staff created a list of 500 terms including different kinds of media, a range of health outcomes, and theories related to the study of media effects. For each citation's record, librarians applied metadata from this list, staff wrote structured abstracts for researchers, and translated the abstract into a plain language summary for non-researchers.

While the Boolean search interface worked, CMCH faced a challenge: How could parents and teachers access research-based information in a way that would take into account their basic search skills and lack of experience with scientific information? Offering the general public a way to ask questions in natural language would allow them to access the scientific research without needing to know how to use Boolean search strategies.

Building the ontology

In Chapter 2, an overview of semantic search using an ontology was presented using the SemanTx Life Sciences semantic search engine as an example. A partnership between CMCH and SemanTx allowed both organizations to apply their knowledge and skills to creating an ontology about the effects of the media on the physical, social, and emotional health of children and adolescents. In this chapter, the ontology building process described in Chapter 4 is revisited, demonstrating the development of an ontology that is currently in use by researchers and the general public through its natural language query interface.

Choosing the source

SemanTx had created an ontology based on the Unified Medical Language System (UMLS), a collection of knowledge sources maintained by the National Library of Medicine that includes a taxonomy and vocabulary focused on the language of biomedicine and health. Since CMCH was focused on the health aspects of media use, the UMLS-based ontology provided an excellent source from which to build the CMCH ontology; only concepts and relationships specific to media would need to be added.

Step 1: Define goals

The goal of the system was to offer users the chance to ask questions in natural language.

Who would be the audience?

- Members of the general public such as parents, teachers and policymakers.

Why would they use this ontology?

- Users will want quick, relevant, evidence-based answers, but may not know how to find that information using a Boolean search method.

What kinds of questions might they ask?

- Depending on their level of expertise, parents might ask the same kinds of questions but phrase them differently, such as:
  - 'Will my teenager be more likely to have sex if he watches a lot of MTV?' Which asks the same question as 'Do music videos encourage sexual behavior in teens?'
  - 'Will watching TV help my daughter learn to read?' Which asks the same question as 'Does television viewing enhance early literacy?'

Step 2: Identify core terms

The CMCH team needed to identify terms related to the study of media effects that were not covered in the UMLS. First, they compared the controlled vocabulary they had already established to the UMLS. Then, the staff selected a number of representative papers about media effects to act as a training set for the Semantic Knowledge Indexing Platform (SKIP) program to index digitally. Running this training set through the indexing platform identified concepts that were well represented in these papers but which were not in the UMLS. For example, media specific terms like 'mean world syndrome' and 'third person effect' were not represented; these would need to be defined and added to the ontology in order for the semantic search process to identify them.

Step 3: Create the taxonomy

The UMLS contains categories for entities such as enzymes, physical objects, and populations groups, but CMCH wanted some more media-specific categories to be added. As shown in Figure 9.2, they defined three new divisions under the category 'Intellectual Product':

- *Media Forms* – Includes types of media that can take on different forms depending on how they are published (e.g. Pornography could be printed or filmed, News could be printed or filmed or broadcast on the radio).
- *Media Types* – Includes major media outlets such as Audio Media (e.g. Radio, Rap Music), Television Media (e.g. Cartoons, Sitcoms), and Print Media (e.g. Magazines, Comic Books).
- *Media Content* – Includes major themes occurring in media that can influence physical, social, or emotional health (e.g. Aggression, Tobacco, Alcohol). They added the parenthetical designation (Media Content) after each term to distinguish it from the health outcomes by the same names.

Figure 9.2 New media categories added by CMCH to the UMLS ontology

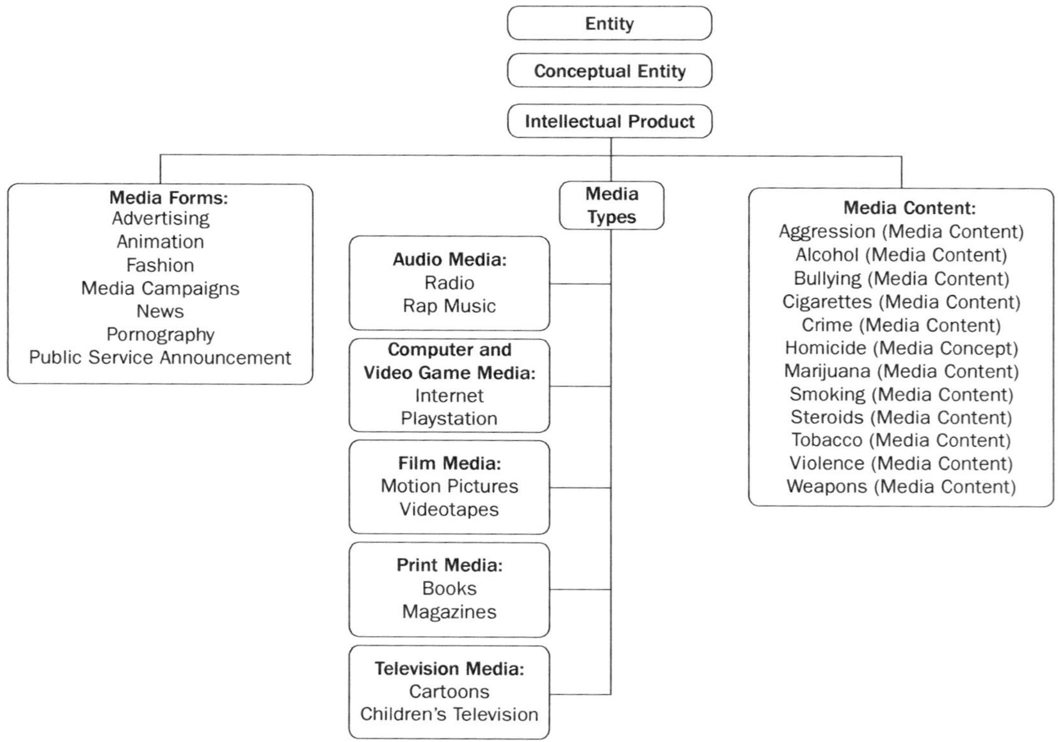

Next, CMCH researchers evaluated the categories where important media terms were assigned, modifying them as necessary. For example, the term Television was listed in the UMLS under the category Manufactured Object. However, the screen, tube, and wiring that made up the object were not as important to the CMCH audience as the way television is used for broadcasting images and stories. Therefore, they moved the term Television to the new category Media Types.

Step 4: Add more terms

Once the categories were established, experts added more terms to each. For example: Newspapers and Comic Books were added to the category Print Media. Sitcoms and MTV were added to the category Television Media.

Step 5: Define terms

Once the terms had been arranged into categories, CMCH staff added definitions by consulting online dictionaries and subject matter experts. When a dictionary offered several senses of a word, they chose the one that best matched the context of the study of media and child health.

Step 6: Add synonyms

Next, staff added synonyms to reflect the many variations of terms. For example, they represented the terms Cinema, Movies, and Film as being the same as Motion Pictures:

Motion Pictures other_name Cinema
Motion Pictures other_name Movies
Motion Pictures other_name Film

After equating all of these terms in the ontology, users would be able to ask their questions using any of those terms and find results containing any of the synonymous terms.

Step 7: Define relationships and use them to make connections

After establishing new categories, terms, and synonyms, defined relationships could be applied to create a profile of semantic relationships. For example, the term Video Games was connected to other terms:

Video Games other_name Electronic Games
Video Games used_for Entertainment
Video Games used_for Military Training
Video Games contain Animation
Video Games rated_by Entertainment Software Ratings Board
Video Games manufactured_by Playstation

Steps 8 and 9: Verify and revise the ontology

Although CMCH did not formally verify the ontology, they were able to make revisions based on queries to the system that did not bring up the expected results. After accessing logs of queries, they could test them out and see the kinds of results users were finding. For example, if someone entered the question 'Will watching TV make my child fat?' and the term *fat* were not an 'other_name' for *overweight* or *obesity* or *weight gain*, then the search engine might not find the appropriate results. Therefore, these terms would need to be revised as synonyms in the ontology.

Because the CMCH staff are so well versed in the literature of this topic, they can automatically recognize when a paper that should be present in the results does not appear. When this occurs, they can analyze which aspect of the question is not appropriately handled in the ontology, and then go back to add relationships and make the ontology understand more clearly what the user is asking.

As new media appear (such as text messaging and blogs), CMCH can add terms to the ontology. As new connections are established through research (for example, research is showing that television affects obesity, though it is not clear just how), CMCH is able to connect concepts in the ontology, modifying how the engine interprets queries and returns results. These updates are made by adding XML tagged elements to the existing ontology, which is time-consuming and laborious, and will hopefully be improved with an easier interface. However, expanding and revising the ontology through any process allows users to ask questions and find answers about current topics, which are often the ones people are most curious to learn more about.

Implementing and comparing to Boolean search

The semantic search engine has achieved its goal; it is successful at interpreting queries no matter how they are worded. 'Do people eat more food when they watch TV?' returns the same set of results as 'How does food consumption differ in the presence of television?' Users can search for information using the vocabulary, lexicon, and structure they are comfortable with to form their question, no matter their level of familiarity with the subject or their level of search experience.

Librarians often ask CMCH staff 'So, which works better? Semantic search or Boolean search?'. After comparing search results from each (King, 2006), CMCH staff learned that both search mechanisms have their strengths and weaknesses. Boolean search is better at returning a comprehensive list of search results, important for those who need total recall such as researchers looking to propose a new study and ensure that the work has not already been completed. The strength of the semantic search is returning accurate answers (no matter how the question is phrased) that are ranked by relevancy. This is important for users from the general public who do not necessarily need every piece of evidence on a topic, but would prefer a quick answer to their question. Realizing that the Boolean and semantic search engines are complementary for the CMCH database, both options are offered so that searchers have a choice of which interface they are more comfortable with, and about the amount and depth of results they want to review for an answer.

The future

CMCH is working with SemanTx to enable new features both for the staff and the users of this semantic technology. For example, the time-consuming nature of writing XML to update the ontology hinders the process of revision. If there were a web interface the CMCH staff could use to easily create new terms and make connections between existing terms, the ontology would be updated more often.

Another exciting feature that may be added is an alerting capability. Users can register queries, then receive emails or RSS updates when new research matching their query is added to the database. In a world where readers expect information to be delivered *to* them, rather than having to search for it themselves, this feature will keep people updated on new research as well as remind them of the resources available from the Center on Media and Child Health.

Overall, the semantic search capabilities for this body of research enable all stakeholders interested in the topic to find scientific evidence on which to base decisions about media use. When people have access to information about this important public health issue, they have an opportunity to make choices that enable children to grow up using the media they are surrounded with in ways that optimize their health and development.

10

Partners HealthCare System: semantic technologies to improve clinical decision support

The health care industry is generating new information at a dizzying pace with no relief in sight. It is an industry with an evolving vocabulary and large amounts of rapidly changing data in the form of patient records, best practice guidelines, new research, and insurance company regulations. For a physician trying to diagnose and treat patients, having access to the right kinds and amounts of information is often a matter of life and death.

At the same time, the evolution of the internet has made new data sources such as clinical studies and current literature more readily available to the general public as well as the medical community, allowing patients to conduct their own research. Although in most cases this is an advantage, because patients are better informed, it can make the health care professional's task more challenging because in the mass of unstructured data on the web, patients are not always referencing the highest quality information. It is clear that physicians need new tools to ensure they access the most authoritative and up-to-date versions of best practice guidelines, diagnostic tests, treatments, and dangerous medication interactions.

In addition to the rapid pace of change and the sheer volume of information, the complexity of integrating different sources of information is exacerbated by the recent rash of mergers and acquisitions across different health care agencies. Hospitals and health care companies find themselves with patient records in different formats, a variety of software tools in use across different locations, and an impressive collection of expertise that the organization does not know how to access. And, of course, there is also the pressure of higher costs and the resulting changes in health care and insurance guidelines. Given all of these complications in health care information, what will it take to provide physicians with the information they require to make the best judgments for their patients? Semantic technology has some answers.

The medical appointment

Let us examine the scene when you arrive at your physician's office with a complaint assuming your physician has all the best tools at her fingertips. When you arrive your physician accesses a summary of your medical record on a large screen; details about each previous visit or condition are available at the click of the mouse. The record provides access to all your current medications, diagnosed conditions, past X-rays, history of blood work, blood pressure, and other test results.

After an interview and examination, your physician interprets your reported symptoms, updates your medical record online, and examines your medical history including related family illnesses in order to make a diagnosis. The computer system then generates a list of the recommended tests to confirm the diagnosis. Your doctor reviews the recommendations and orders appropriate diagnostic tests, and your referrals are automatically processed.

When you return after the tests are completed, the doctor has your medical record on screen and your recent test results are highlighted. Authoritative up-to-date information regarding treatments, warnings, and drug interactions are displayed so that your physician can focus her attention on selecting the best treatment for your diagnosis. After eliminating some of the possibilities, your doctor reviews the recommended treatment options and examines possible dangerous drug interaction warnings before prescribing a treatment tailored to your individual needs. The selected treatment plan, including prescriptions, is printed for you, reducing the possibility of medication error due to a doctor's handwriting!

The system described, a *clinical decision support* system, organizes and presents to your physician the best medical information available – a bit like having an entire team of experts in the room. It reminds the clinical staff about tests that should be performed regularly and alerts the physician about drug interactions. All of this information is currently available electronically in one form or another, in one place or another, within our current health care system; the challenge is bringing it all together in a timely fashion and understandable form.

One major health care company has emerged as a leader in the use of semantic technologies to meet these challenges. The Partners HealthCare System is a major health care company made up of thousands of clinical, research, and support staff at hospitals, community health centers, rehabilitation and hospice centers, and research institutes. The Clinical Informatics Research and Development (CIRD) group within the Partners system has a mission 'to improve the quality and efficiency of care for patients at Partners HealthCare by assuring that the most advanced current knowledge about medical informatics (clinical computing) is incorporated into clinical information systems...' (Clinical Informatics Research

& Development, 2008a). Within CIRD, the Clinical Knowledge Management and Decision Support (Clinical KMDS) Group is responsible for the infrastructure that makes this knowledge available to clinicians. As an active member of the World Wide Web Consortium's (W3C's) Semantic Web HealthCare and Life Sciences Interest Group since its inception in 2005, Clinical KMDS has shared its exploration of ontologies and semantic technology through its publications and presentations on topics such as the role of semantic technologies in translational medicine (Hongsermeier, 2006), functional taxonomies and rule-based systems (Wright et al., 2007), and implementable clinical guidelines (Kashyap, Morales, and Hongsermeier, 2005). As a result of their progress, Partners clinicians have the tools to make the best decisions possible for their patients' welfare.

Partners HealthCare System's solution

Knowledge management

The sheer volume of information available within the Partners network provides a significant knowledge management challenge, which has been further complicated by mergers and acquisitions resulting in multiple data centers, isolated collections of data (*data silos*), and a number of independent information technology (IT) groups. The Clinical KMDS team, tasked with providing the infrastructure for providing access to this knowledge, looked first at the data sources within the network to provide an inventory of *knowledge assets* (Hongsermeier, Kashyap, and Sordo, 2007). The size and complexity of the enterprise was reflected in the physical and logical organization of the data, which was hiding behind a diverse collection of software tools. To further complicate matters, although many applications were web-enabled, the information was not easily shared across the enterprise.

To address the challenges of sharing data across Partners HealthCare System, Clinical KMDS conceived of an internal portal, which would provide access to the vast repository of knowledge and provide the tools for improved clinical decision support. The information was in the form of application-specific content, such as documentation templates and reports, observation catalogues, order sets, rules, reminders, and drug interaction information. There was also a notably large amount of knowledge contained in vocabularies used throughout the system (Hongsermeier, Kashyap, and Sordo, 2007). The vocabularies and knowledge assets contained references to concepts, relationships, and rules that could be used to develop an effective ontology for clinical decision support. Key factors in creating a long-term plan included a shared repository, a content management system, a common vocabulary, and the ability to create and interpret rules.

Organizing the extensive collection of knowledge sources is a daunting task, but Partners has already made great progress in this area. Clinical KMDS began by modeling the knowledge categories using a limited number of relationships, for example: subclass, has_patient_age_group, and has_content_type. This enabled staff to derive a 'knowledge taxonomy to tag, aggregate, and organize information' (Hongsermeier, Kashyap, and Sordo, 2007). An important next step was to decide how new information would be entered into the system. Previously existing editors, some of which were application-specific, were being used to add new content. Partners integrated its knowledge taxonomy into these editors so that new content would be added based on a foundation of robust semantics. Partners is currently in the process of mapping its internal knowledge assets to industry standard vocabularies, expanding its taxonomy even further. Integrating all of these existing knowledge sources across the enterprise by connecting them with relationships and other semantic properties is making it easier to locate and make use of the resources available throughout the system.

Another important component of clinical decision support that can be aided by semantic technology is the plethora of clinical guidelines used by physicians to direct treatment of many common conditions. For example, the American Diabetes Association recommends the following regarding the prevention and management of diabetes:

> Lower triglycerides to <150 mg/dl (1.7 mmol/l) and raise HDL cholesterol to >40 mg/dl (1.15 mmol/l). In women, an HDL goal 10 mg/dl higher (>50 mg/dl) should be considered. (American Diabetes Association, 2007)

This guideline may be translated into two parts, the antecedent (if) and consequent (then):

> *IF* patient has diagnosis of diabetes *AND* patient is female
> *THEN* lower triglycerides to <150 mg/dL *AND* raise HDL cholesterol to >50 mg/Dl
> *IF* patient has diagnosis of diabetes AND patient is male
> *THEN* lower triglycerides to <150 mg/dL *AND* raise HDL cholesterol to >40 mg/Dl

Doctors often must memorize thousands of clinical guidelines in order to determine how and when to treat a patient. Many different software applications have attempted to capture and make these guidelines available to clinicians to reduce the amount of memorization needed. Thus, when the guidelines *are* available electronically, they are often embedded in various applications and accessible using different techniques. Guidelines are often more effectively encoded as rules, as illustrated above, but different terminology can complicate the process of executing rules.

Ontologies provide a solution to both parts of this problem: concepts and synonyms provide a way to understand terminology, and *inference* provides the mechanism for executing rules. An ontology could infer two types of facts:

- A patient condition can be inferred based on current medical record information.
- Diagnostic tests or therapeutic interventions can be recommended based on a patient condition.

At Partners, projects are currently under way to extract the rules from various applications so that they may later formally become part of an ontology; this will enable the system to keep up with changing vocabulary and guidelines more easily (Hongsermeier, Kashyap, and Sordo, 2007).

The Partners' medical appointment: SmartForms

As a result of their progress in knowledge management and the application of semantic technologies, Partners' clinicians have many of the tools envisioned in our opening medical appointment scenario through the use of a web-based application called SmartForms, which provides 'integrated advanced decision support' (Postilnik et al., 2006). Figure 10.1 shows an image provided by Clinical KMDS at Partners

Figure 10.1 SmartForm from Partners HealthCare System

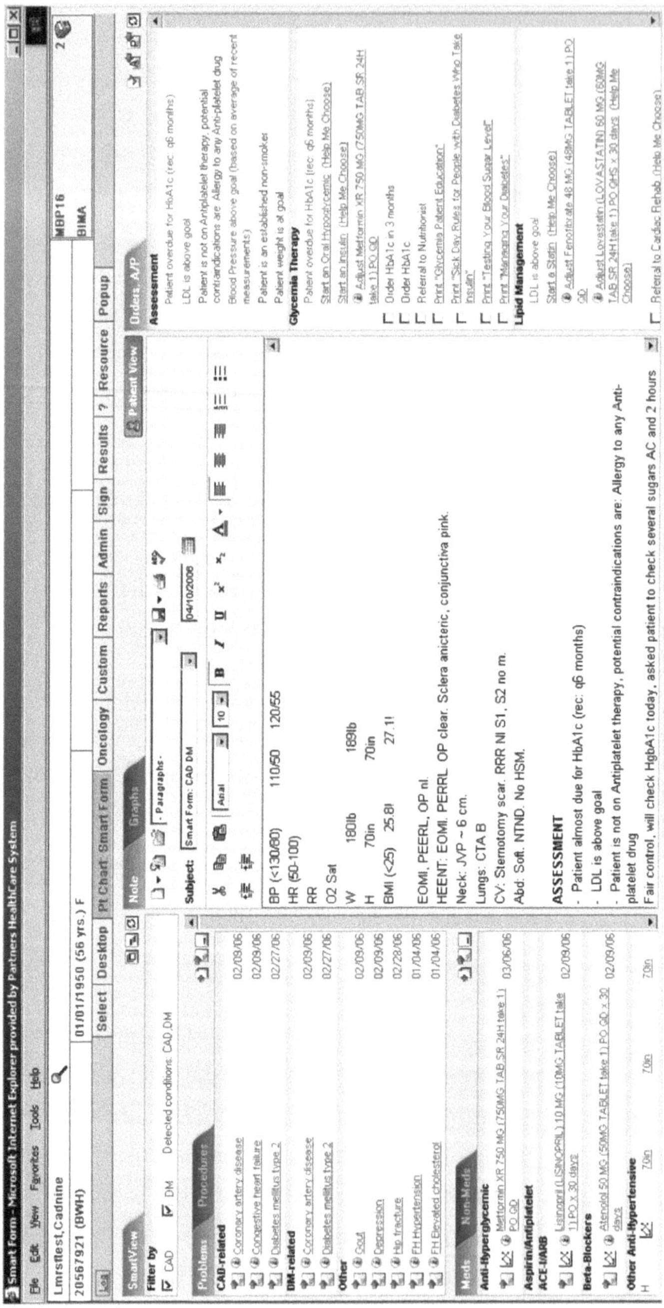

Source: Clinical KMDS at Partners HealthCare

HealthCare as an illustration of a SmartForm. No information contained in it is to be considered as medical advice or a recommendation. When a patient arrives in a Partners HealthCare physician's office, the SmartForm application is launched, providing details from the patient's electronic medical record, including problems, medications, allergies, etc.

In the left column, the SmartForm displays diagnoses, medications, procedures, allergies, and a history of vital signs taken at previous appointments. When the physician clicks on the information buttons (*i*) to the left of any of the items in this list, a search is executed in Partners' reference sources such as UpToDate or Micromedex, providing the most current information for the diagnosis or medication. In the center, a screen is available for the physician to enter notes from today's visit. In the right column, reminders, diagnostic tests (order sets), and treatment options are displayed based on the patient's medical record. The assessment box in the top right displays a summary; items displayed in red require attention. The items requiring attention for this patient are that:

- she is overdue for an HbA1c test of glucose levels
- LDL is above goal
- blood pressure is above goal.

Additional details are provided below the items in red. The physician is presented with suggestions regarding glycemia therapy because the patient is overdue for glucose level testing; options include providing the patient with educational material about glycemia and diabetes, and testing blood sugar. The lipid management section suggests that the patient should start a statin or adjust other medications. The physician could also order tests directly from this screen or print educational material for the patient.

Though our society often places value on a doctor's memory, experience, and ability to remember details in order to diagnose and treat disease, SmartForm displays patient information to assist physicians so that they do not have to rely *solely* on their memories and experiences. With SmartForms, the clinician reviews a patient's history, conditions, and test results on a single page, and then may compare effectiveness, contraindications, side effects, and drug interactions involved in various treatments, allowing the selection of the safest and most effective treatments. Physicians still discuss symptoms, perform examinations, and make diagnoses, but they are aided by semantic technology. This semantically powered clinical decision support system provides value every day to clinical staff, helping physicians better provide patients with the best health care.

Lessons learned

When Clinical KMDS began, staff were faced with a tangle of knowledge sources, some overlapping, some even contradictory. Knowledge was tightly bound to applications and managed by different groups, used for different purposes, and located in different departments. In order to make changes that were consistent across all of these sources, the knowledge editors needed to work together to modify each data source manually. Today's system allows online collaboration among subject matter experts to define new knowledge, manages the acquisition of knowledge assets using a standard taxonomy, and provides critical decision support based on the patient's medical record and knowledge assets.

Two strategies enabled Clinical KMDS to learn about the knowledge available across the Partners network: Clinical KMDS performed a comprehensive inventory and conducted user interviews to understand the current processes for adding new content to the system. This led to the tactical decision to manage knowledge acquisition though the use of a controlled vocabulary, the knowledge taxonomy. It was also determined that providing access to the large collection of knowledge assets required flexible search capabilities. To ensure integration of the knowledge assets in clinical decision support, Partners identified a need to agree on definitions for concepts such as diseases, drugs, contraindications, and complications (Kashyap et al., 2005). A taxonomy of clinical decision support methods has been defined based on the functional needs of a clinical decision support system (Wright et al., 2007), which automates generation and rendering of precise relevant clinical content. What did staff learn along the way?

Take an inventory

Although a painstaking process, taking a comprehensive inventory of existing knowledge assets allowed the team at Partners to identify the wide variety of information already available. By avoiding the temptation to immediately define an ontology at the start, they discovered that managing the acquisition of knowledge would be critical to their success. They also recognized that much of the value embedded in the system was in the form of rules. By addressing the organization and acquisition of knowledge first, Clinical KMDS had the advantage of understanding the concepts at the core of the knowledge assets before attempting to finalize concept definitions. Recognizing that facts were embedded in knowledge assets and applications, they determined that extracting the rules would ultimately allow them to manage changes to rules more effectively. Taking an inventory early in the process helped Partners to define a better strategy for achieving their goals.

Derive use cases

Use cases are detailed step-by-step descriptions of tasks performed by users. User interviews are conducted to elicit a user's needs, and in the process the vocabulary of the domain is identified and the most important aspects of a system from the user's perspective are elucidated. Use case analysis provides the most effective method for developing a user-centric system and provides an excellent foundation for reflecting the vocabulary of a domain.

Standardize vocabulary

As Partners began the task of organizing the knowledge for a clinical decision support system, they developed a standardized vocabulary in the form of the knowledge taxonomy. Over time, Partners expects to incorporate structured knowledge objects such as concepts, relationships, and rules, and even more complex objects such as a condition that is defined by multiple symptoms and test results. Such objects will likely require more complex knowledge structures such as ontologies that support complex relationships, constraints, and inference, and can manage versions of objects. Standardizing vocabulary allowed Partners to organize existing information, provide editors for knowledge acquisition, and better manage integration of knowledge assets into clinical decision support.

Provide flexible search capabilities

Clinical KMDS provides multiple types of search strategies so that users can find information quickly. Guided navigation allows the user to click through taxonomy levels; filters permit the user to select characteristics such as specific groups within the Partners network (hospitals, community health centers), clinical disciplines (dermatology, surgery), content type (pdf, word document), or populations (geriatric, pediatric); and a basic keyword search is also provided. But importantly, Partners recognized that even more flexible techniques are necessary. They have provided a 'mixed mode' search where users can combine filter-based and guided navigation to narrow a search further. Certainly, our earlier examples of semantic search might provide a good alternative as well for Partners, but in the meantime the flexible techniques provided enable users to find knowledge more effectively than ever before.

The future

One of the current knowledge management tasks for Clinical KMDS is aligning its knowledge assets with industry and federal terminology standards. For example, staff are mapping their internal knowledge assets to various standard vocabularies such as ICD-9 codes used for insurance billing. They also continue to review and update existing knowledge assets, such as the medication knowledge and drug interaction knowledge bases (Clinical Informatics Research & Development, 2008b). In clinical decision support, the group is extending its functional taxonomy to other institutions to measure its effectiveness in different settings and to incorporate additional decision support information (Wright et al., 2007).

A longer term objective and major challenge ahead is to more uniformly manage changes to knowledge assets. That is, as new information becomes available, content, taxonomies, concepts, relationships, definitions, and rules must all be updated. The process of knowledge acquisition must be capable of propagating changes throughout the system rapidly and reliably so that modifications do not need to be made manually on so many levels.

The exponential growth in information about genomics and health care must be communicated to physicians as they diagnose and treat patients. As medicines are discovered, as new techniques replace old ones, as information about genetics brings to light new strategies for treatment, physicians will increasingly be unable to store and keep current their wealth of knowledge by themselves. Partners will leverage new genomic and phenotype information through its alliance with Harvard Partners Center for Genetics and Genomics (Hongsermeier, Kashyap, and Sordo, 2007).

Clinical KMDS maintains a vast array of clinical decision support content within the Partners HealthCare network used by thousands of health care workers. The decision support system informed by this content serves to notify physicians of scheduled events such as annual tests, to advise physicians regarding possible dangerous drug interactions or ineffective treatments based on genetic information or family history. The clinical decision support system of tomorrow will offer personalized medicine based on an immediate response to new patient information and the most up-to-date clinical trial results, treatments, and genomics information; physicians will have all the best tools and most up-to-date information available to provide patients with the best chance of living a healthy life.

11

MINDSWAP: using ontologies to aid terrorism intelligence gathering

September 11, 2001 – a date that irreversibly changed our world. It was a defining moment; events are even marked by whether they occurred pre- or post-9/11. In light of subsequent investigations that uncovered extensive intelligence information available *before* the attack, it is alarming that intelligence agencies were unable to detect the plot in advance.

These are some of the facts that were known:

- The CIA knew that two of the hijackers, Khalid Almihdhar and Nawaf Alhazmi, had ties to Osama bin Laden because they both had attended an al-Qaida summit in Malaysia in 2000 (CBS News, 2002b).
- The CIA was aware that Khalid Almihdhar held a US B-1/B-2 multiple-entry visa (Hill 2002).
- Alhazmi and Almihdhar used their real names on flight lesson appointments and car registrations in California (Treverton, 2004).
- On January 4, 2001, the FBI determined that Khallad bin Atash had been a principal planner in the Cole bombing (Gilmore, 2002). Atash was also know to have been at the Malaysia meeting with Almihdhar and Alhamzi (Finn, 2002).

- On July 10, 2001, Phoenix FBI agent Ken Williams wrote a memo to FBI headquarters, warning of the possibility that bin Laden's followers were attending US flight schools in preparation for terrorist attacks (CBS News, 2002a).
- In late August 2001, Almihdhar tried to book a reservation with his real name on the American Airlines website for his 9/11 flight, but his request was denied because his address could not be verified. He ended up purchasing his ticket with cash at the American Airlines counter on September 5, 2001 (Meuller III, 2002).

How did we miss the connections between all of these facts? The volume of information available and the restricted ability of our agencies to share information between themselves made it difficult. How can semantic technologies help put these kinds of pieces together to make intelligence gathering more robust?

Intelligence agencies collect and create an astounding number of documents including everything from digital records such as computer files, emails, web pages, news reports, and spreadsheets to hand-written reports and recorded conversations. Making connections among these various pieces of information is challenging when the items number in the hundreds; when the items are in the hundreds of thousands, it is nearly impossible, as we learned after 9/11.

When a counter-terrorism analyst keeps track of these relationships between people, times, places, and financial transactions, he or she often relies on the same mishmash of methods mentioned above, using everything from formally kept digital records to highlighted papers and sticky notes. After combining all of his resources including both publicly available and classified information, CIA case officer Robert Baer said that his charts 'started to look like the wiring diagram for a Boeing-747 cockpit' (Baer, 2002). It was likely that only Baer could understand the different lines, abbreviations, and colors he employed to make connections and distinctions in those charts. These kinds of notes limit collaboration between analysts because they require lengthy explanation by the note-taker himself, and because they are in a physical form that cannot be accessed by many people at the same time. The notes are also of limited value to future analysts because they are crafted with a specific purpose in mind. As we shall see, semantic technology offers solutions.

At the University of Maryland, a group called MINDSWAP (Maryland Information and Network Dynamics Lab Semantic Web Agents Project) created a web portal aimed at solving many of these problems for analysts. Their work aims to explore the use of ontologies to represent terrorist activity, which is often composed of 'a small group of people carrying out a complex chain of actions and bound by an intricate web of relationships' (Mannes and Golbeck, 2005). If intelligence analysts can readily see connections between people, locations, and transactions, they may be able to resolve questions about how terrorist cells are organized.

Building, using and maintaining the ontology

Building the MINDSWAP ontology took a team of people from various backgrounds, including a terrorism analyst/ subject expert who knew what kind of information needed to be represented and had a vision of improving how he usually worked, programmers to make his vision come alive, and undergraduate research assistants to enter the relationships that he wanted to express. The MINDSWAP team needed to clarify what the goals of the ontology were so that they could tailor the structure to their needs. They knew they could not represent *all* intelligence about terrorism, so they decided to focus their efforts on strategic intelligence (information about groups, leaders, policies, and structure) rather than on tactical intelligence (how specific attacks were launched) (Mannes and Golbeck, 2007). The result is a web portal called Profiles in Terror (PiT; *http://profilesinterror.mindswap.org*), showing connections between people involved in terrorist activities.

Since the focus was to be on connections and relationships between humans, it was very important to create categories and properties that allowed for each person in the ontology to be described thoroughly, including their permanent characteristics (height and birth date) and their transitory characteristics (weight, location, and name). As is a problem with the creation of all ontologies, they struggled with the balance between it being comprehensive enough to include a variety of data, but not so broad that they had to develop a more complex system of categories than necessary. The ontology is made up of 70 different classes and 173 properties (Mannes and Golbeck, 2005).

When a person's name is added to the ontology, it is first placed in a category such as diplomat, criminal, terrorist, non-terrorist, politician, or tribal/ethnic group leader. Then relationships are used to link each person with characteristics such as where they went to school, who they lived with, what cities they traveled through, where they attend religious services, whom they contacted, which crimes they were involved in, and other properties that might put them in specific places at specific times.

A representation of the PiT taxonomy, determined by using the browse function on the PiT website, is reproduced in Figure 11.1.

In the diagram, Babar Ahmed and Shadi Abdullah are classified as terrorists. Let us say the staff of MINDSWAP

Figure 11.1 **A representation of the PiT taxonomy**

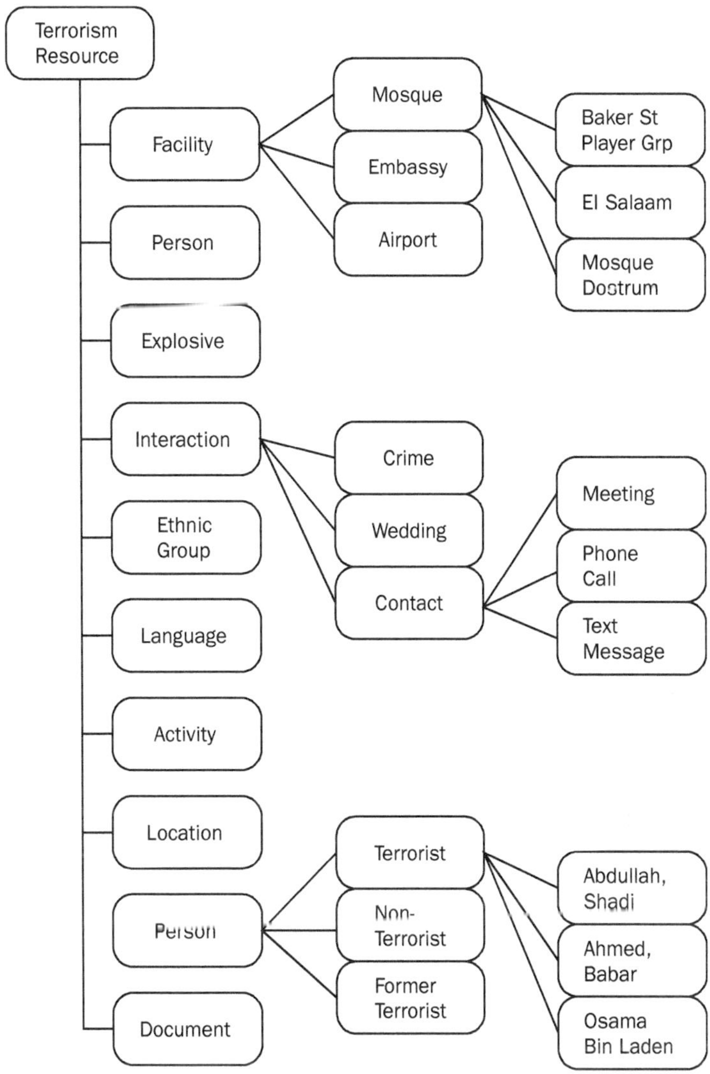

comes across intelligence about Ahmed and add the following relationships to the ontology:

> Babar Ahmed member_of Mosque Dostrum
> Babar Ahmed part_of Phone Call on May 28, 2007

A month later, a different analyst learns that Abdullah had a documented interaction on May 28, 2007, and enters the following relationships:

Shadi Abdullah member_of Mosque Dostrum
Shadi Abdullah attendance_at Meeting on May 28, 2007
Shadi Abdullah part_of Phone Call on May 28, 2007

Though the entries for Ahmed and Abdullah occurred at different times and by different people, the ontology will recognize a connection between the two terrorists worthy of pursuing. Perhaps Abdullah and Ahmed know each other from Mosque Dostrum. Perhaps Abdullah attended a meeting on May 28, 2007, after which he called Ahmed to relay critical information. The analyst viewing these connections 'has the best of both worlds. A view can simply connect individuals on the bases of shared life experiences (every person who attended a university) or can provide more comprehensive views of their activities' (Mannes and Golbeck, 2007).

MINDSWAP has entered semantic connections for one of the most famous terrorists, Osama Bin Laden. His information is listed under 'OBL' and his page includes a photo, a list of properties, and a visual representation of his semantic connections. Some of the relationships on the page include:

OBL given_name Osama Bin Laden
OBL nickname Abu Abdullah
OBL place_of_birth Riyadh, Saudi Arabia
OBL affiliation Al-Qaida

Aside from the personal information entered above, MINDSWAP staff were able to enter specific information about contact he had with others and events he attended:

OBL organizer Mughniyah OBL meeting
OBL involved_person Abu Doha-OBL meeting
OBL involved_person Azzam is OBL's teacher in Jeddah

Once several people's profiles are rounded out, the semantic web portal can physically represent the extensive web of connections between Bin Laden and others (Figure 11.2).

The MINDSWAP ontology is constantly evolving as new information comes to light and new cases need to be followed. Programmers created a user interface called SWOOP so that subject experts can easily add to and edit the ontology on their own (Kalyanpur, Parsia, and Hendler, 2005).

Another impressive power of the ontology is the ability to infer relationships based on information supplied. For example, if:

Person A has_uncle Person B
Person B has_son Person C

then the ontology can infer that Person A and Person C are cousins. This is especially helpful when tracking the complex web of terrorist groups since, as there is often an information overload, analysts may have overlooked key connections.

The ability to include maps and photographs is another key feature of the Profiles in Terror ontology. Though a relationship may be textually expressed between a terrorist living in one city and his suspected involvement in a major event in another city, the ability to attach maps to each location may lead the analyst to realize the proximity between these two cities and come to new conclusions. Photos are also a critical addition to the ontology. Photos placing individuals together at a certain time and place,

Figure 11.2 **Representation of the connections between Bin Laden and others**

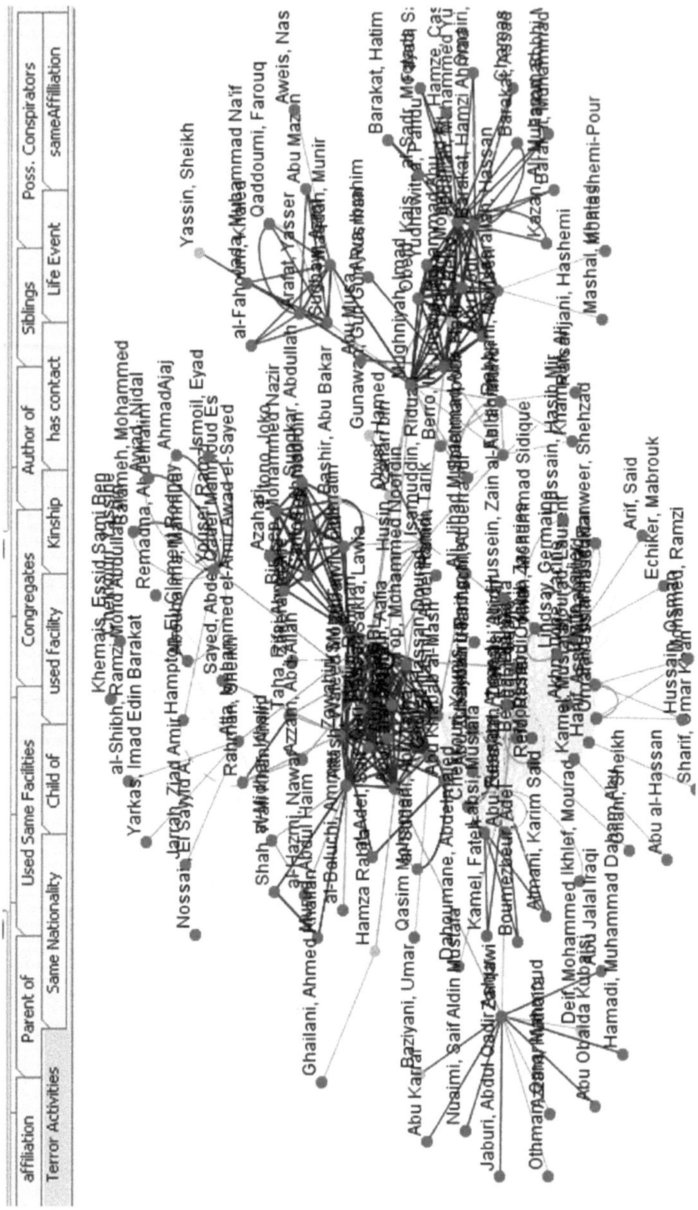

Source: *http://profilesinterror.mindswap.org/document/11/OBL*

photos of graffiti (often used to mark territory), and images of scanned documents all help analysts visualize the situations they attempt to understand (Mannes and Golbeck, 2005).

Sharing information with other experts

MINDSWAP allows members of the general public to register for a free account, which enables them to comment on different relationships and people in the ontology. In order to maintain quality control, only MINDSWAP staff can alter the ontology, but allowing others to comment provides for an interactive discussion between analysts who may have more or different information to add based on their own research.

MINDSWAP also offers free downloads of the ontology and of the SWOOP editor. Since the best ontologies are those focused on a narrow subject, MINDSWAP wanted other analysts to be able to take the basic structure of the ontology and customize it for their own use. 'This means that users can select sets of statements that reflect their personal interests, even if no one else has had that specific focus' (Mannes and Golbeck, 2005). For example, many terrorist organizations, such as Fuerzas Armadas Revolucionarias de Colombia (FARC), are hierarchical and have very carefully defined roles. MINDSWAP has not added this kind of hierarchy to their ontology because their analysts focus their efforts on a variety of groups, some of which are not structured that way. However, the ontology's basic structure could be downloaded from MINDSWAP and the organizational charts of FARC could be added for analysts focusing all of their effort on that region.

The future

What is next for the Profiles in Terror ontology? MINDSWAP hopes to improve SWOOP, their ontology editor, so that subject experts can directly establish relationships without needing the help of programmers. The easier it is for additions and changes to be made to the ontology, the more up to date and useful it will be.

Although the graphical representations of connections between *people* are satisfactory, the staff hope to improve the representation of connections between *events*. Tracking events over time is a significant challenge for MINDSWAP. Though staff have the ability to choose a format for how time codes will be recorded, it will need to be in one consistent manner. This poses problems because if they choose to represent time as day/month/year, then they will need to fit all of their information to that format. But if they know that a terrorist moved from one city to another during the spring of 1998, and it does not particularly matter for intelligence reasons which *day* he moved on, then they are forced to choose a day and month to fit the time code format.

In some cases an analyst wants to track a particular person's movement over the course of one day, meaning that the time code would need to reflect hours and minutes within a day. But in most cases, they rarely have access to information that detailed. So although the ability to represent people and events over time would be a very useful improvement to the system, it remains a challenge to figure out the nuts and bolts of making it work.

For now, MINDSWAP staff continue to use, add to, and improve their ontology to streamline the discovery of connections between people and events, helping to aid counter-terrorism analysts as they pursue a real understanding of how terrorists operate.

Part 4
Advanced topics

Part 4 provides a more detailed overview of the languages in which ontologies can be expressed and the tools that can be used to create them. Some readers may have enough of an overview at this point to skip this section and return to it at a later time.

12

Languages for expressing ontologies

Ontologies need to be expressed in standardized ways so that computers can understand their structure and interpret the meaning behind the concepts expressed. Several computer-readable languages have emerged that allow for definitions of the ontology components of categories, concepts, relationships, and rules. The eXtensible Markup Language (XML) was the first structured language explicitly designed for sharing documents on the World Wide Web. However, as noted in Chapter 6, XML is limited in its ability to address relationships and semantics. The Resource Description Framework (RDF) uses XML syntax to impose additional structure on the documents it describes. The additional structure enforces semantic consistency and provides user-defined relationships, many-to-many relationships, and built in rules. RDF is not a language, but an application built in XML. However, RDF does not fully support the concept of *identity*, that is, knowing whether or not two different things are the same. This is important in evaluating semantic capabilities to express synonymous relationships. The Web Ontology Language (OWL) fully supports this capability. The Simple Knowledge Organization System (SKOS) is a simple schema expressed in RDF that provides a simpler mechanism for defining other knowledge structures.

In their book, *Ontologies for Bioinformatics*, Ken Baclawski and Tianhua Niu make the case that an ontology can be represented in many different ways from a flat file to OWL-Full (Baclawski and Niu, 2006). The question is, which of these languages is most appropriate for the effective use of your particular ontology? There are, of course, dissenting opinions on this topic, and thus you will find ontologies expressed in different languages. For example, the Gene Ontology is available in several flat file formats as well as RDF-XML, OWL, a relational database format, and others (Gene Ontology Consortium, 2008). The following sections will provide a description of the most common languages for expressing ontologies.

XML

The eXtensible Markup Language (XML), introduced in 1996, was intended to provide a universal language for describing web documents (Connolly, 2003). For example, a book contains a chapter and a chapter is made up of paragraphs. The XML representation of a book declares each part of the book. XML *elements* are contained within angle brackets and offer essential information:

```
<elementName>elementValue</elementName>
<author>Charles Darwin</author>
```

An element may also have *attributes* that offer further description but are not essential; elements may have any number of attributes:

```
<elementName attrName= ‘attrValue’>elementValue
</elementName>
<author gender= ‘male’>Charles Darwin</author>
```

This is how one paragraph of the book *With Malice Toward None: A Life of Abraham Lincoln* (Oates, 1994) would be expressed in XML:

```
<?xml version='1.0'?>
<book>
<title>With Malice Toward None</title>
<subtitle>A Life of Abraham Lincoln</subtitle>
<author>Stephen B. Oates</author>
<chapter title='Rivers of Time'>
<para>Outside of Illinois, people knew little about
him. Even newspapers were ....</para>
...
</chapter>
...
</book>
```

A document type definition (DTD) defines the elements and attributes permitted within an XML file. A DTD for the book example above might look like this:

```
<!– DTD example to define a book –>
<!ELEMENT book (title, (subtitle)?, (author)+, (chapter)+)>
<!ELEMENT title (#PCDATA)*>
<!ELEMENT subtitle (#PCDATA)*>
<!ELEMENT author ((personname)*))>
<!ELEMENT chapter ((para)+)>
<!ATTLIST chapter title CDATA>
<!ELEMENT para (#PCDATA)*>
</dtd>
```

In this DTD, a book has a title, an optional subtitle (optional is symbolized by the question mark), and one or more authors (one or more is symbolized by a plus sign), followed by one or more chapters. A chapter comprises one attribute, title, and one or more paragraphs; a paragraph is PCDATA which is simply a string of characters. (For our purposes both CDATA and PCDATA can be considered character data.)

XML imposes constraints on the structure and data types in a document, that is, it assures that all elements required are present, that they are in the correct order, and that data designated as character data is indeed character data. This makes XML an excellent tool for describing hierarchies or taxonomies. However, its limitations for describing more complex structures became more clear as people attempted to use XML to describe ontologies. XML Schema (XMLS) was developed in 2001 to 'provide a means for defining the structure, content and semantics of XML documents' (World Wide Web Consortium, 2008). Although it is possible to express a simple ontology in XML or XMLS, neither of these languages are able to capture the complexity of the relationships or semantics required to describe adequately most useful ontologies (Baclawski and Niu, 2006).

RDF

The Resource Description Framework (RDF) was first defined in 1997 (Herman, Swick, and Brickley, 2007). RDF 'is a language for representing information about resources in the World Wide Web' (Manola and Miller, 2004). This sounds very similar to the goals for XML and the distinction between the two has been cause for much discussion (Berners-Lee, 1998). As Dan Brickley reported, 'RDF's contribution is simple. When we see XML files written according to the RDF specifications, we know how to *interpret* them' (Brickley, 2001). In other words, RDF provides meaning – provides semantics. Although RDF does allow us to express semantics, it is limited in a fundamental requirement of 'understanding' – the ability to state explicitly that two resources are identical.

A resource is anything that can be named on the web; it is named by a universal resource identifier (URI). In RDF, concepts are defined as resources and relationships are defined as *predicates* (also called properties). The underlying structure in RDF could be viewed as a representation of a fact. It is represented in the form of a *triple*, which identifies a subject, predicate, and object:

Joe	married_to	Susan
Subject	Predicate	Object

RDF Schema (RDFS) is a language for describing RDF documents. (Recall that XML has two description languages – DTD and XMLS.) RDF supports several built-in rules about hierarchical relationships, extending hierarchy rules to properties of concepts as well as to concepts themselves; for example 'subClassOf' and 'subPropertyOf' are transitive. This allows us to infer new facts or information. For example, if Joe is married_to Susan and Susan is daughter_of Ellen, then we can infer that Ellen is Joe's mother-in-law.

Here is an RDF example of the record for the book mentioned previously:

```
<rdf:RDF xmlns:rdf='www.w3.org/1999/02/22-rdf-
syntax-ns#'
xmlns:dcterms='http://purl.org/dc/terms/'
xmlns:ex=http://mysite.org/taxonomy/>
```

```
<rdf:Description rdf:about='http://example.org/123'>
<dcterms:title xml:lang='en'>With malice toward none:
the life of Abraham Lincoln </dcterms:title>
<dcterms:creator xml:lang='en'>Oates, Stephen B.
</dcterms:creator>
<dcterms:type xml:lang='en'>text</dcterms:type>
<dcterms:publisher xml:lang='en'>London; Boston:
Allen & Unwin, </dcterms:publisher>
<dcterms:date xml:lang='en'>1978, c1977. </dcterms:date>
<dcterms:language xml:lang='en'>eng</dcterms:language>
<dcterms:description xml:lang='en'>Includes bibliographical
references and index. </dcterms:description>

<dcterms:subject xml:lang='en'>
 <rdf:Description>
<dcam:memberOf rdf:resource='http://mysite.org/ taxo
nomy/vocab'/>
<rdf:value>Lincoln, Abraham, 1809-1865. </rdf:value>
 </rdf:Description>
</dcterms:subject>
<dcterms:subject xml:lang='en'>
<rdf:Description>
<dcam:memberOf rdf:resource='http://example.org/
taxonomy/vocab'/>
<rdf:value>Presidents–United States—Biography. </rdf:
value>
</rdf:Description>
</dcterms:subject>

<dcterms:identifier xml:lang='en'>
 </rdf:Description>
</rdf:RDF>
```

OWL

Since 2004 the W3C has been actively working on a web ontology language (OWL) (World Wide Web Consortium, 2004a). It is designed specifically to meet the needs of the World Wide Web. OWL's syntax is nearly identical to RDF's, but OWL is intended to better describe the semantics (relationships, definitions, and rules) of concepts and to allow inference of new data based on these semantics. There are three variations on OWL: *OWL Lite* is the most restrictive of the three; *OWL DL* (OWL Description Logic) supports inference and additional relationships; and *OWL Full*, which imposes virtually no constraints, and provides the ability for the user to extend the language itself. Nearly all ontologies described in OWL today use either OWL Lite or OWL DL.

SKOS

The Simple Knowledge Organization System (SKOS) is a simple schema expressed in RDF for defining thesauri, taxonomies, classification schemes, and subject headings. It is intended to address two levels of complexity: the OWL language itself, and the ontology. By providing a simple language with which to define knowledge structures that are simpler than ontologies, this effort is intended to facilitate movement towards the semantic web. SKOS defines concepts, preferred and other names ('prefLabel, altLabel'), and simple relationships such as *broader*, *narrower*, and *related* relationships. Document properties include: *scopeNote* and *definition*. Inference rules are also supported and may be expressed in several ways, but a number of the features required to fully support semantics and ontology building are missing. Nonetheless, SKOS may meet the requirements for users seeking to be prepared for the semantic web.

Figure 12.1 shows a SKOS representation of an extract from the UK Archival Thesaurus (UKAT), a controlled vocabulary used by archivists for indexing.

Figure 12.2 shows the entry as a diagram; concepts are represented in circles and relationships are represented by the arcs.

Figure 12.1 **Extract from UK Archival Thesaurus represented in SKOS**

```
Term: Economic cooperation

Used For:
    Economic co-operation

Broader terms:
    Economic policy

Narrower terms:
    Economic integration
    European economic cooperation
    European industrial cooperation
    Industrial cooperation

Related terms:
    Interdependence

Scope Note:
Includes cooperative measures in banking, trade,
industry etc., between and among countries.
```

Source: *http://www.w3.org/TR/swbp-skos-core-guide/#secaboutexamples*

Figure 12.2 Extract from UK Archival Thesaurus represented as a diagram

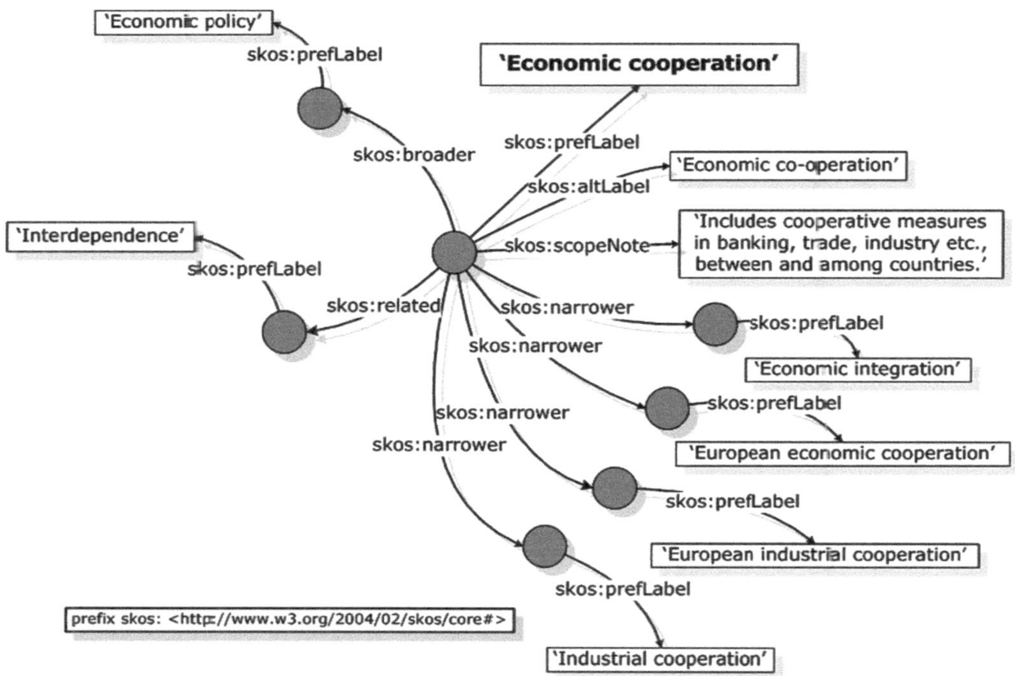

Source: *http://www.w3.org/TR/swbp-skos-core-guide/#secaboutexamples*

Ontology language features – comparison chart

Table 12.1 summarizes several important features of languages that may be used to describe ontologies or other knowledge structures. This section provides some useful guidelines for selecting an appropriate ontology language. The column definitions are as follows:

- *Concepts* specifies whether or not the ontology language supports defining concepts.
- *Relationships* identifies the type of relationship that is supported by the language. *Containment* is another way to express the parent–child or superclass–subclass relationship. Some languages allow users to define their own relationships, which provides the maximum flexibility for support of complex semantics. Languages sometimes use different terminology to express a relationship; this information is provided in the chart.
- *Constraints* denotes whether the language supports constraining the values to specific sets or ranges. They guarantee that information makes sense, for example ensuring that the value for the author concept is limited to a person's name.
- *Inference/Rules* indicates whether or not the language supports the ability to infer new facts from existing information.
- *Properties/Attributes* describes how properties or attributes for elements are expressed in the language.
- *Comments* provides miscellaneous information including in many cases what type of knowledge structure the language is best suited to describe, whether or not the

order of elements is significant, or special characteristics of the language. Order is significant in the following XML example:

<concept>
<name='Macintosh apple'>
<is-a='apple'/>
</concept>
is not the same as
<concept>
<is-a='apple'/>
<name='Macintosh'/>
</concept>.

Table 12.1 Features of languages that may be used to describe ontologies or other knowledge structures

Language	Concepts	Relationships	Constraints	Inference or rules	Properties or attributes	Comments
XML	Yes	Containment only	No	No	No	Represents taxonomies well; order is significant.
XML Schema	Yes	Containment only	Yes, data types and ranges of values. For example, the concept of human age is constrained to be a number between 0 and 150.	No	No	Represents taxonomies well; order is significant.
RDF	Yes	Yes, expressed as a 'triple': subject, verb, object	Yes	Built-in rules only	Yes (called resources)	Order of elements within a concept/object does not matter. In the example above, RDF recognizes these as two representations of the same concept.

Table 12.1 Features of languages that may be used to describe ontologies or other knowledge structures (*Cont'd*)

Language	Concepts	Relationships	Constraints	Inference or rules	Properties or attributes	Comments
RDF Schema (RDFS)	Yes	Yes, between concepts (called classes in RDFS)	Yes	Built-in rules only; supports hierarchies for properties as well as classes	Yes, resources may be used to define characteristics, such as a range of values for classes and properties.	Order of elements within a concept or property does not matter.
OWL Lite	Yes	Between properties and classes	Yes. More precise constraints than RDFS; for example, in some cultures, a man may have 'exactly one' wife at any specific moment.	Built-in rules only; supports hierarchies	Yes, richer types of properties than RDFS, and characteristics of properties are supported; for example, the human body has symmetry.	

Table 12.1 Features of languages that may be used to describe ontologies or other knowledge structures (*Cont'd*)

Language	Concepts	Relationships	Constraints	Inference or rules	Properties or attributes	Comments
OWL DL	Yes	Between properties and classes	Yes, additional built-in constraints may be used.	Yes; permits the inference of new facts from existing information.	Yes	Adds the capability of reasoning; allows a class or concept to have many parents in a hierarchy.
OWL Full	Yes	Between properties and classes	Yes	Yes	Yes	No computational guarantees, which means that there is no guarantee that execution of a rule will complete. This also introduces the idea that a fact may be undecidable, that is, there may not be enough information available to infer a fact.

Table 12.1 Features of languages that may be used to describe ontologies or other knowledge structures (*Cont'd*)

Language	Concepts	Relationships	Constraints	Inference or rules	Properties or attributes	Comments
SKOS	Yes	Yes, but not defined by the user of SKOS. There is a set of defined semantic relationships that are supported: broader, narrower, broader transitive, narrower transitive, related, member, mapping relation, etc.	No	No	A pre-defined set of attributes is supported. They include document properties such as scopeNote, definition, example.	SKOS offers an RDF language that is simpler to use but more limited than OWL. It is able to express knowledge organization structures (KOS) such as taxonomies, thesauri, etc. Note that SKOS also supports mapping between two different KOS in a simple way. SKOS is an OWL-full ontology. No formal semantics.

13

Tools for building ontologies

An ontology can be expressed in structured languages such as XML or RDF, but as the ontology develops and grows larger, maintaining the structure of these knowledge sources quickly becomes overwhelming and difficult to manage. Tools for building ontologies attempt to simplify the task of creating and using an ontology. Most tools provide some ability to visualize the relationships among concepts and nearly all can generate the ontology into two or more ontology languages.

An online survey of tools in 2002 reported on 56 ontology building tools (Denny, 2002). In a 2004 update of this same survey, 94 tools were identified (Denny, 2004). With so many tools available and new ones appearing frequently, this book will not attempt to provide a comparison between them, but rather mention a number of tools, and focus on recommending criteria to consider when choosing a tool for building ontologies. When you are ready to select a tool, be sure to search online for new developments.

Protégé is one of the most well-known tools, created by the Stanford Center for Biomedical Informatics Research and supported by grants from the National Library of Medicine, Defense Advanced Research Projects Agency, eBay Inc., and the National Science Foundation, among others (Protégé, 2008). Protégé supports the creation, visualization, and management of ontologies in a number of formats and allows the user to export ontologies into OWL, RDF Schema, XML, and other language formats. As this tool was first mentioned in the literature in the mid to late 1980s, it has clearly withstood the test of time, evolving with new advances in technology and ontology development. Since Protégé is a free open-source ontology editor, downloading it is a great way to start learning more about what an ontology building tool can do. Figure 13.1 shows an example of the restaurant ontology created in Chapter 3 as it would be shown in Protégé.

Other well-known ontology development tools include the Integrated Ontology Development Environment (IODE) from Ontology Works Inc., Ontolingua from Stanford, IBM's Integrated Ontology Development Toolkit, and OBO-Edit, developed by the Berkeley Bioinformatics and Ontologies Project.

Generally the best tool for building an ontology is the simplest one that can handle the work you need done. If the ontology is small, a simple visual editor may be all that is required. If the ontology will change often with current literature, a more complex tool will be required, perhaps one that has the capability of learning from submitted documents to make suggestions and improvements. Additionally, if the ontology is large and many relationships exist, the visual representation may become such a complicated diagram that it is more difficult to read than a text description. As previously stated, tools appear and disappear often from the market so it is valuable to focus on the criteria that allow you to choose the best tool for your specific project.

Figure 13.1 Example of restaurant ontology built using Protégé

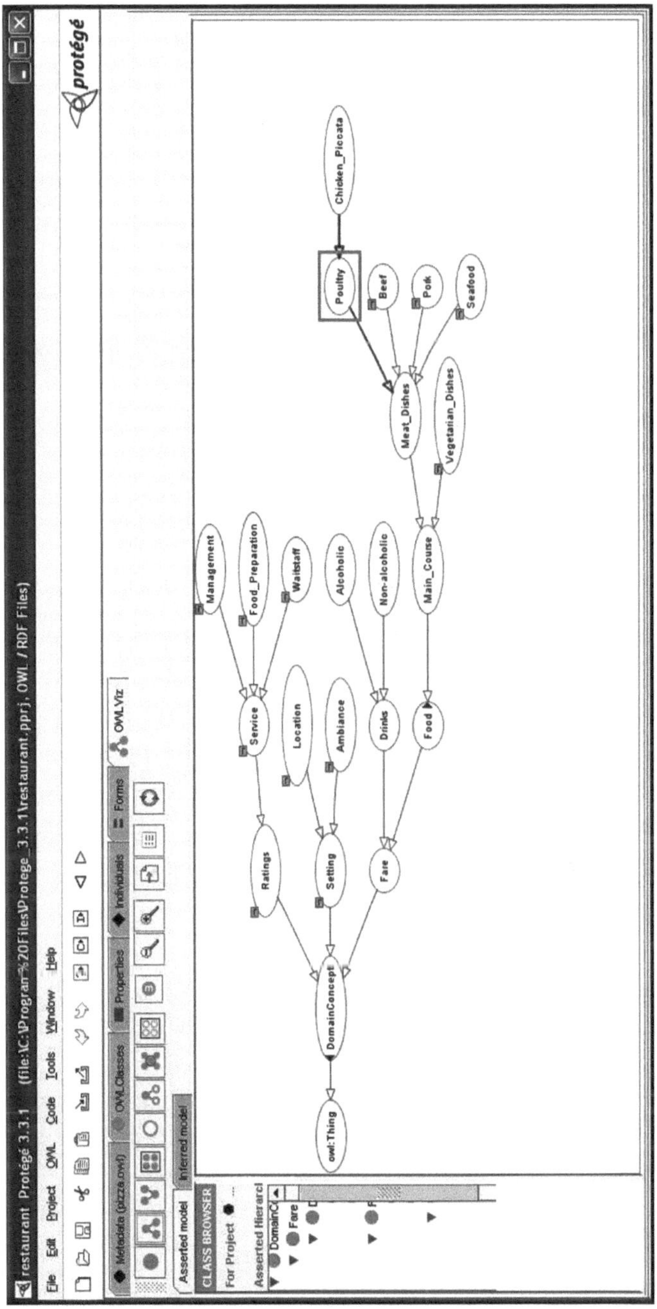

Basic criteria when evaluating ontologies

Usability

Usability is defined by what is intuitive and simple for the user. Look for a tool that provides the basics in a straightforward way. Keep in mind the steps it takes to build an ontology – you need to define a taxonomy of categories, name concepts that fit into each of these categories, add synonyms, and then define relationships between them. This much should be easy and straightforward in any tool.

Ease of navigation and visualization

If the purpose of your ontology is to allow your users to navigate through concepts and relationships on their own to find information, visualization is likely very important. Navigating through a graphical image of the taxonomy is a nice feature; the visualization is difficult if the tool attempts to show large sections of the ontology at once, with all the relationships. A better choice would be a visualization tool that permits the user to select specific relationships to model or simply lists the concepts within categories.

Extraction and learning capabilities

Tools that extract information from documents to help identify concepts of an ontology will be a good choice if your ontology is continually developing and current literature is readily available. For this feature, look for natural language parsing capabilities for extraction. Generally, a selection of documents that are considered representative of the domain are selected and submitted for linguistic analysis. This is called a 'training set'. Linguistic tools can analyze this content in order to synthesize ontology terms, which can then be reviewed by experts for inclusion into the ontology. Some tools provide this as an automated feature.

Languages supported

As detailed in the previous chapter, there are a number of languages used for expressing ontologies; this is still an active area of development and identifying a tool that will keep up with changes is important. Choose a tool that exports multiple formats in multiple languages, including at least XML, RDF or RDF Schema, and OWL.

Version control

Ontologies, by nature, are always an unfinished product; if they are to stay relevant knowledge sources, they must evolve as the literature and vocabulary of a domain evolves. Maintaining proper version control will enable you to better manage changes to your ontology.

Check validation and consistency

As ontologies grow larger and more difficult to view on a single page, the chance of having inconsistencies and invalid relationships increases. Some tools provide automated validation or consistency checking. For example, they will notify you if cyclic relationships are found; this is where concept X is a subclass of another concept Y, which is a subclass of the original concept X. Though this seems improbable, a large ontology can contain mistakes such as these that would be important to catch before other software based on the ontology is running.

Part 5
Transitions to the future

We have learned much about how semantics and ontologies are transforming the next version of the web. But how do we as librarians progress from learning about the basics to developing and encouraging the full vision articulated by Berners-Lee?

In our final chapter, we will examine the challenges and opportunities that the future holds, from immediate plans to long-term visions of the semantic web.

14

Challenges and opportunities: using semantics today

In May 2001, *Scientific American* published 'The Semantic Web', Tim Berners-Lee's first article about his vision of the next version of the internet. In this article, Berners-Lee describes a futuristic scenario where a woman at a doctor's office initiates a series of activities from her handheld browser to arrange for a specialist, physical therapy, and transportation for her mother. The automated series of activities includes:

- retrieving the treatment recommended from the doctor
- consulting with health insurance for approved providers in the local area
- comparing these providers against a rating service to determine the best people to care for the woman's mother
- checking schedules for all parties so that transportation is provided for each visit. (Berners-Lee, Hendler, and Lassila, 2001).

This idea of making hyperlinks meaningful, that is attaching semantics to data and links on the web, seems simple, and had occurred to Berners-Lee in his youth. As of 2006, this idea 'remains largely unrealized' (Shadbolt, Hall, and Berners-Lee, 2006), but progress has been made.

The World Wide Web Consortium (W3C), an organization with over 400 members, has defined standards to enable the connections on the web and the creation of ontologies to power the semantic web. This has fostered an active network of early adopters. In a 2007 article, 'The Semantic Web In Action' (Feigenbaum et al., 2007), authors present a selection of case studies and announce: 'The enabling technologies have come of age.'

Although the use of ontologies is growing, there are concerns about the challenges presented in using ontologies. In Tim Berners-Lee's initial article about the semantic web (Berners-Lee, Hendler, and Lassila, 2001), it is clear that the role of the ontology is critical. Ontologies define the semantics and enable complex tasks to be performed automatically. This may lead to the expectation that once the ontologies are developed, the fully functional semantic web will be available. As discussed in this book, rapid progress has been made in tools for building ontologies as well as other applications of semantic technologies. Some practical concerns remain though.

Challenges

Ontologies are difficult to build and require a significant investment of time, effort, and resources.

In Chapters 3 and 4, readers saw the step-by-step process of building an ontology. Even representing a simple and common topic such as food or recipes is a significant undertaking and most ontologies are being built around highly complex topics that evolve rapidly. Involving subject matter experts, librarians, and programmers to make the best ontology possible requires not only that they fully support the idea, but that their time is directed away from other activities and paid for using financial resources. As Martin Hepp of the Digital Enterprise Research Institute points out, 'Unfortunately, for many domains, whether the gain in automation enabled by an ontology outweighs the resources necessary for creating it remains a completely open research question' (Hepp, 2007). While the best ontologies deeply explore a limited scope of knowledge, this means that the potential audience of users for each ontology is small. A more broadly applicable ontology would either generate a large and unwieldy ontology and create significant technical challenges or possibly force a shallow treatment of the domains, creating an ontology of little value. An alternative approach is to add another layer of semantics that connect related terms across multiple ontologies; an approach called mediation, which is discussed below.

Can we keep up with how quickly knowledge evolves?

Managing change is difficult. In some fields, the rapid changes to vocabulary and rate of discovery demand that changes be propagated accurately and rapidly. How do we manage change in a controlled and efficient manner? Standards must be set to ensure that there is a formal process for additions and deletions of concepts and relationships, but these standards must not be so strict that they unnecessarily hinder those changes from happening at a reasonable pace.

Library of Congress Subject Headings are an example of a controlled vocabulary that rarely changes. Any proposed changes must be submitted to the Program for Cooperative Cataloging and reviewed. Catalogers are cautioned that because changes involve so much work, they 'should consider the impact of such a change and be judicious in recommending one' (Program for Cooperative Cataloging,

2008). In her article 'Charting a Changing Language with LCSH' Lynn El-Hoshy notes that:

> During the era of the card catalog, a conservative approach was taken to changing headings because of the cost of revising catalog cards and then refiling them at the Library of Congress and elsewhere... A watershed of sorts was marked in 1987 when a decision was made to cancel the heading 'Moving-pictures' in favor of 'Motion Pictures', even though that change involved revising authority records for approximately 400 related headings and updating the subject headings assigned to thousands of catalog entries (El-Hoshy, 1998).

Changes to an ontology are easier to make because they are most often built electronically. Changes can be made to one area and automatically updated throughout a system; indexed files can be re-indexed by a machine. However, standards for change still need to exist in order to ensure that they are warranted and based on evidence within the field and the impact and cost of changes must be evaluated.

What strategies can help to mediate among different ontologies?

This issue is not limited to ontologies; many controlled vocabularies differ and the strategy thus far has been to provide mappings from a term in one vocabulary to a term in another. In order for the semantic web to be fully interoperable, ontologies must be able to talk to each other. As Jos de Buijn points out, ontology mediation is making relationships between ontologies explicit so that if an application is not familiar with one ontology, it may be able to relate to it through the use of an already familiar ontology connected to it (de Bruijn, 2004).

The strength of ontologies lies in their ability to explore deeply a domain from the perspective of experts in a field. However, even expert definitions and relationships can differ depending on what discipline the ontology comes from. For example, an ontology that contains the term 'ice' may bring to mind different things for different users, all of which are correct. For an anthropology scholar of Caribbean culture, 'ice' may connect to concepts such as refrigeration and storage of food while an environmentalist may connect the term 'ice' with Antarctica, permafrost, and glaciers. If these two ontologies were able to be mediated, the meaning of the word 'ice' would grow exponentially and the other words around it would give it the appropriate meaning for the context. This combination of data would provide a rich user experience where the user benefits from many simultaneous ways of looking at the world of information. The challenges of ontology mediation are far from being solved and more research is needed here to define appropriate answers.

What semantic tools are available?

This is a challenge with any new technology. Some of the current tools are disjointed and require significant integration work, others are able to provide a complete package when needs are modest. Each year's Annual International Semantic Web Conference includes a challenge for people to develop new semantic tools that can be used on the open web, rather than made specifically for an enterprise solution. These tools must be created for end-users, must make use of the meanings of data, and must be able to work with more than one set of data. The 6th Annual Conference in 2007 had 19 entries, including tools with trends such as improving user interface and providing easy ways to group similar concepts (Zaino, 2007). This emphasis on tailoring tools for ontology creators adds significantly to the possibility of creating more and better ontologies. Aaron Mannes, creator of the previously detailed Profiles in Terror ontology, comments that 'Until the non-computer science specialists are able to construct useful ontologies, the semantic web will not fulfill its potential' (Mannes and Golbeck, 2007). Though there is not a unified plan for tool development, we can be sure that with the active semantic community at work, tools will continue to evolve to meet user needs.

Are collaborative efforts a possibility?

Since creating and maintaining an ontology is a significant undertaking, one might wonder about combining efforts into collaborative projects. Certainly, since a variety of skills are needed and useful in ontology creation (subject expertise, librarianship, programming, etc.), collaboration is absolutely necessary on some level. However, there are examples of projects that go beyond their immediate enterprise. As mentioned in Chapter 8, the Biogen Idec Case Study, their group is hoping to form a consortium with other experts to flesh out a more complete thesaurus for the biomedical community.

The idea of collaboration on a broader scale may not be as welcome as the collaboration of experts of a domain. Web 2.0 has been rife with collaboration efforts such as the process of formalizing a user-created encyclopedia (Wikipedia) and encouraging tagging of websites (del.icio.us), books (LibraryThing), and photos (Flickr). With credibility given to everyone's version of knowledge and organization, no matter their qualifications, these efforts have proven to be popular but are generally considered to lack authority.

Where do librarians fit into the semantic web vision?

If one of the goals of ontologies is to provide an underlying structure for the semantic web to operate, thus allowing users to ask natural language questions, then the obvious question for librarians is: What will my role be if I am not helping to provide answers to patrons? Just as catalogers help to create and apply the standardized classification system to materials in order for patrons to be able to find them independently, librarians can take an active role in the creation and maintenance of ontologies. Most librarians are skilled at being able to look at a corpus of knowledge (whether contained in books, journals, or digital formats), establish categories, arrange the information from general to specific, and find connections between various areas of that corpus. These are the exact skills required to build an ontology.

In the past few decades, librarians have established a reputation for being avid followers and adopters of new technology, able to take popular applications and customize them for use by a library. The technical skills required for this range from simple facility with computers to the ability to develop databases. Because of this technical knowledge, librarians are often able to converse well with staff in information technology departments, programmers, and software developers, making them ideal candidates for acting as liaisons between the subject experts and computer programmers required to establish these complex systems needed for the semantic web.

First steps toward achieving the vision

Given the amount of unorganized electronic data available on the web, and the rapid pace of proliferation, the semantic web is the only viable option for making sense of it all. Instead of waiting for the arrival of the semantic web, start joining in the movement by either learning more about these topics or deriving value from today's technology:

- Read about semantic technologies and other related issues using the additional resources in the appendix of this book.
- Seek out conferences, workshops, and presentations by librarians and non-librarians to learn more about how these technologies are being applied in the library world, in academia, the military, and business.
- Keep up with developments in semantic technology by looking at news from the W3C and from blogs about these topics.
- Use RDF or SKOS to define taxonomies and thesauri in use. This will facilitate sharing and the electronic use of these knowledge structures.
- Investigate Protégé or another free ontology builder. Build a small ontology to get better acquainted with how to apply the structure to a limited set of concepts.
- When choosing new technology, investigate semantic options. Many search engines, data mining tools, and authoring systems currently utilize semantic technologies.

Whether you take an active approach by engaging yourself, your library, or your patrons in this movement, or you simply read more about semantics and ontologies, you will be keeping your knowledge current by following semantic web developments. And as with all technologies, those who are able to keep up with developments are those who are most likely to become early adopters, to have suggestions for improvement, and become leaders as the promise of the shift from the World Wide Web to the semantic web is realized.

Appendix: Additional resources

Historical perspective

Copeland, Jack, and Diane Proudfoot (2008) 'The Turing Archive for the History of Computing'. University of San Francisco, Department of Computer Science. Available at *http://www.cs.usfca.edu/www.AlanTuring.net/turing_archive/index.html*. Accessed on February 23, 2008.

Sowa, John F. (2005) 'Building, Sharing, and Merging Ontologies'. Available at *http://www.jfsowa.com/ontology/ontoshar.htm*. Accessed on February 18, 2008.

von Neumann, John (1958) *The Computer and the Brain*. New Haven, CT: Yale University Press.

Semantic web

Berners-Lee, Tim (1999) *Weaving the Web: The Original Design and Ultimate Destiny of the World Wide Web by Its Inventor*. New York: HarperCollins Publishers Inc.

Berners-Lee, Tim, James Hendler, and Ora Lassila (2001) 'The Semantic Web'. *Scientific American Magazine*, 284.5: 34–43. Available at *http://www.sciam.com/article.cfm?articleID=00048144-10D2-1C70-84A9809EC588EF21*. Accessed on March 8, 2008.

Feigenbaum, Lee, et al. (2007) 'The Semantic Web In Action'. *Scientific American Magazine*, 297.6: 90–7.

Greenberg, Jane, and Eva Méndez, eds. (2007) *Knitting the Semantic Web*. Binghamton, NY: Haworth Information Press.

World Wide Web Consortium (2008) 'World Wide Web Consortium'. W3C. Available at *http://www.w3.org/*. Accessed on February 23, 2008.

Ontologies

Baclawski, Kenneth, and Tianhua Niu (2006) *Ontologies for Bioinformatics*. Cambridge, MA: MIT Press.

Di Maio, Paola (2007) 'Ontology: Making the Business Case'. *Business Intelligence*, 7.7.

Gene Ontology Consortium (2008) 'Gene Ontology'. Open Biomedical Ontologies. Available at *http://www.geneontology.org*. Accessed on February 18, 2008.

Hepp, Martin (2007) 'Possible Ontologies: How Reality Constrains the Development of Relevant Ontologies'. IEEE Computer Society. Available at *http://www.heppnetz.de/files/IEEE-IC-PossibleOntologies-published.pdf*. Accessed on February 18, 2008.

Noy, Natalya F., and Deborah L. McGuinness (2001) *Ontology Development 101: A Guide to Creating Your First Ontology*. Stanford, CA: Standford University. Available at *http://www-ksl.stanford.edu/people/dlm/papers/ontology-tutorial-noy-mcguinness.pdf*. Accessed on March 8, 2008.

Natural language parsing

Association for the Advancement of Artificial Intelligence (2007) 'Natural Language Processing'. AAAI. Available at *http://www.aaai.org/AITopics/html/natlang.html*. Accessed on February 18, 2008.

Charniak, Eugene (1997) 'Statistical Techniques for Natural Language Parsing'. *AI Magazine*, 33–44.

Coxhead, Peter (2001) 'An Introduction to Natural Language Processing (NLP)'. University of Birmingham, Department of Computer Science. Available at *http:// www.cs.bham .ac.uk/~pxc/nlpa/2002/AI-HO-IntroNLP .html*. Accessed on February 18, 2007.

Jurafsky, Daniel, and James H. Martin (2000) *Speech and Language Processing: An Introduction to Natural Language Processing, Computational Linguistics, and Speech Recognition*. Upper Saddle River, N.J.: Prentice-Hall.

Manning, Christopher D., and Hinrich Schütze (1999) *Foundations of Statistical Natural Language Processing*. Cambridge, MA: MIT Press.

Ontology languages and tools

XML

World Wide Web Consortium (2008) 'Extensible Markup Language (XML)'. W3C. Available at *http://www.w3.org/ XML/*. Accessed on February 18, 2008.

RDF

Brickley, Dan (2001) 'Understanding RDF'. European Commission Metadata Workshop. Available at *http://ilrt .org/discovery/2001/01/understanding-rdf/*. Accessed on February 18, 2008.

Herman, Ivan, Ralph Swick, and Dan Brickley (2007) 'Resource Description Framework (RDF)'. World Wide

Web Consortium. Available at *http://www.w3.org/RDF/*. Accessed on October 8, 2007.

Miller, Eric (1998) 'An Introduction to the Resource Description Framework'. *D-Lib Magazine*, May. Available at *http://www.dlib.org/dlib/may98/miller/05miller.html*. Accessed on March 8, 2008.

OWL

Herman, Ivan (2006) 'Web Ontology Language (OWL)'. World Wide Web Consortium. Available at *http://www.w3.org/2004/OWL*. Accessed on February 18, 2008.

SKOS

Miles, Alistair, and Sean Bechhofer (2008) 'SKOS Simple Knowledge Organization System Reference'. World Wide Web Consortium. Available at *http://www.w3.org/TR/skos-reference/*. Accessed on February 18, 2008.

Ontology building tools

Denny, Michael (2004) 'Ontology Tools Survey, Revisited'. XML.com. Available at *http://www.xml.com/pub/a/2004/07/14/onto.html*. Accessed on February 18, 2008.

Biogen Idec

Davies, Kevin (2006) 'Search and Deploy'. *Bio-IT World*, October 16: 24–33. Available at *http://www.bio-itworld.com/issues/2006/oct/biogen-idec*. Accessed on March 8, 2008.

Havenstein, Heather (2007) 'IT Execs Seek New Ways to Justify Web 2.0'. *Computerworld*, August 13. Available at *http://www.computerworld.com/action/article.do?command=viewArticleBasic&articleId=300310*. Accessed on March 8, 2008.

Hayes, William (2007) 'Just Enough, Just in Time'. *BI Review Magazine*, December 3. Available at *http://www.bireview.com/bissues/2007_36/10000468-1.html*. Accessed on March 8, 2008.

Roberts, Phoebe (2006) 'Turn STOP Words into GO Words and PARAGRAPHS into GRAPHS: The Power of Text Analytics'. The Pharmaceutical and Health Technology Division Annual Spring Meeting: 'Collaboration: Combining Efforts for Improved Results'. Memphis, TN. Available at *http://units.sla.org/division/dpht/meetings/spring2006/2006-roberts.pdf*. Accessed on March 8, 2008.

Roberts, Phoebe M. (2006) 'Mining literature for systems biology'. *Brief Bioinform*, 7.4: 399–406.

Roberts, Phoebe M., and William S. Hayes (2008) 'Information Needs and the Role of the Text Mining in Drug Development'. *Pacific Symposium on Biocomputing*, 13: 592–603. Available at *http://psb.stanford.edu/psb-online/proceedings/ psb08/roberts.pdf*. Accessed on March 8, 2008.

Wiegler, Laurie (2007) 'OHSU Proposes Wiki-Styled Thesaurus for Relationship-Oriented Text Mining'. *BioInform*, May 25.

Center on Media and Child Health

King, Brandy E. (2006) 'Boolean vs. Semantic Search Interfaces: Which Work Better?' *Special Libraries Association Annual Conference*, Baltimore, MD: SLA

Contributed Papers. Available at *http://www.sla.org/PDFs/2006CPKing.pdf*. Accessed on March 8, 2008.

King, Brandy E., Sharon Gray, and Michael Rich (2005) 'Center on Media and Child Health: Building an E-Resource for Researchers and the Public'. Paper presented at the Special Libraries Association Annual Conference, Toronto, Ontario. SLA Contributed Papers. Available at *https://www.sla.org/Documents/conf/toronto/King.doc*. Accessed on March 8, 2008.

Partners HealthCare

Glaser, John, and Tonya Hongsermeier (2007) 'Managing the Investment in Clinical Decision Support'. In *Clinical Decision Support: The Road Ahead*, ed. Robert A. Greenes. Boston, MA: Elsevier Academic Press, 403–22.

Hongsermeier, Tonya, Vipul Kashyap, and Margarita Sordo (2007) 'Knowledge Management Infrastructure: Evolution at Partners HealthCare System'. In *Clinical Decision Support: The Road Ahead*, ed. Robert A. Greenes. Boston, MA: Elsevier Academic Press, 447–68.

Hongsermeier, Tonya (2006) 'From the Bench All the Way to Bedside Clinical Decision Support: The Role of Semantic Technologies in a Knowledge Management Infrastructure for Translational Medicine'. World Wide Web Consortium. Available at *http://www.w3.org/2001/sw/hcls/f2f-2006/presentations/Semantic%20Web%20 Bench %20to%20 Bedside.ppt*. Accessed on February 17, 2008.

Kashyap, Vipul, and Tonya Hongsermeier (2005) 'Towards a National Health Knowledge Infrastructure (NHKI): The Role of Semantics-based Knowledge Management'. World Wide Web Consortium. Available at *http://www*

.w3.org/2005/04/swls/White_Paper.pdf. Accessed on February 18, 2008.

Kashyap, Vipul, et al. (2005) 'TaxaMiner: An Experimentation Framework for Automated Taxonomy Bootstrapping'. *International Journal of Web and Grid Services*, special issue on semantic web and mining reasoning. Available at *http://lsdis.cs.uga.edu/~cartic/publications/TaxaMiner IJGWS.pdf*. Accessed on March 8, 2008.

Kashyap, Vipul, Alfredo Morales, and Tonya Hongsermeier (2005) 'Creation and Maintenance of Implementable Clinical Guideline Specifications'. World Wide Web Consortium. Available at *http://www.w3.org/2005/04/swls/clinical_guidelines.pdf*. Accessed on February 17, 2008.

Kashyap, Vipul, et al. (2005) 'Definitions Management: A Semantics-based Approach for Clinical Documentation in Healthcare Delivery'. *Lecture Notes in Computer Science*, 3729: 887–901. Available at *http://www.w3.org/2005/04/swls/iswc_final_submission.pdf*. Accessed on March 8, 2008.

Kashyap, Vipul, Tonya Hongsermeier, and Samuel Aronson (2004) 'Can Semantic Web Technologies Enable Translational Medicine? (Or Can Translational Medicine Help Enrich the Semantic Web?)'. World Wide Web Consortium. Available at *http://www.w3.org/2005/04/swls/Semantic_Web_Translational_Medicine.pdf*. Accessed on February 18, 2008.

Wright, Adam, et al. (2007) 'A Description and Functional Taxonomy of Rule-based Decision Support Content at a Large Integrated Delivery Network'. *Journal of the American Medical Informatics Association*, 14.4: 489–96.

MINDSWAP and Profiles in Terror

Golbeck, Jennifer, Aaron Mannes, and James Hendler (2005) 'Semantic Web Technologies for Terrorist Network Analysis'. In *Emergent Technologies and Enabling Policies for Counter Terrorism*, eds. Robert Popp and John Yen. Hoboken, NJ: IEEE Press.

Mannes, Aaron, and Jennifer Golbeck (2007) 'Building a Semantic Web Portal for Counter Terror Analysis'. *Proceedings of the IEEE Aerospace Conference*, March, 1–5.

Mannes, Aaron, and Jennifer Golbeck (2005) 'Building a Terrorism Ontology'. MINDSWAP. Available at *http://mindswap.org/papers/TerrorOntologyfinal.pdf*. Accessed on June 16, 2007.

Semantic technology vendors

Ontology building tools

Protégé: *http://protege.stanford.edu*
Ontolingua: *http://www.ksl.stanford.edu/software/ontolingua*
Chimaera: *http://www.ksl.stanford.edu/software/chimaera*

Semantic search solutions

CognitionSearch: *http://www.cognitionsearch.com*
EasyAsk: *http://www.easyask.com*
Lexalytics: *http://www.lexalytics.com*
Linguamatics: *http://www.linguamatics.com*
Nervana: *http://www.nervana.com*
SemanTx: *http://www.semantxls.com*
TextPresso: *http://www.textpresso.org*

Bibliography

Abney, Steven Paul (2006) 'CASS Partial Parser'. Available at *http://complingone.georgetown.edu/~linguist/parser.html*. Accessed on April 4, 2008.

American Diabetes Association (2007) 'Standards of Medical Care in Diabetes – 2007'. *Diabetes Care*, 30 suppl 1: S4–41. Available at *http://care.diabetesjournals.org*. Accessed on March 8, 2008.

Angell, Marcia (2005) *The Truth About the Drug Companies: How They Deceive Us and What to Do About It*. New York: Random House.

Baclawski, Kenneth, and Tianhua Niu (2006) *Ontologies for Bioinformatics*. Cambridge, MA: MIT Press.

Baer, Robert (2002) *See No Evil*. New York: Crown Publishers.

Bender, Emily M. (2001) 'Linguistics 290A/1: Corpora on corpus.linguistics.berkeley.edu'. University of California Berkeley. Available at *http://corpus.linguistics.berkeley.edu/corpora_on_corpus.html*. Accessed on February 18, 2008.

Berners-Lee, Tim (1998) 'Why RDF Model is Different from the XML Model'. World Wide Web Consortium. Available at *http://www.w3.org/DesignIssues/RDF-XML.html*. Accessed on February 18, 2008.

Berners-Lee, Tim (1999) *Weaving the Web: The Original Design and Ultimate Destiny of the World Wide Web by Its Inventor*. New York: HarperCollins Publishers Inc.

Berners-Lee, Tim, James Hendler, and Ora Lassila (2001) 'The Semantic Web'. *Scientific American Magazine*, 284.5: 34–43. Available at *http://www.sciam.com/article.cfm?articleID=00048144-10D2-1C70-84A9809EC588EF21*. Accessed on March 8, 2008.

Brickley, Dan (2001) 'Understanding RDF'. European Commission Metadata Workshop. Available at *http://ilrt.org/discovery/2001/01/understanding-rdf/*. Accessed on February 18, 2008.

Burnard, Lou, and C. M. Sperberg-McQueen (2006) 'TEI Lite: Encoding for Interchange: An Introduction to the TEI Revised for TEI P5 release'. Text Encoding Initiative. Available at *http://www.tei-c.org/release/doc/tei-p5-exemplars/html/teilite.doc.html*. Accessed on February 18, 2008.

Carr, Eve (2007) 'Dining at Joe Fortes Makes You Feel Like a Star'. Suite101.com. Restaurant Review. Available at *http://www.suite101.com/article.cfm/gourmet_passport/95253*. Accessed on January 13, 2007.

CBS News (2002a) 'Bush Opposes 9/11 Query Panel'. May 23. Available at *http://www.cbsnews.com/stories/2002/05/15/attack/main509096.shtml*. Accessed on February 18, 2008.

CBS News (2002b) 'Hijackers Lived With FBI Informant'. September 9. Available at *http://www.cbsnews.com/stories/2002/09/09/attack/main521223.shtml*. Accessed on February 18, 2008.

Charniak, Eugene (1997) 'Statistical Techniques for Natural Language Parsing'. *AI Magazine*, 33–44.

Clinical Informatics Research & Development (2008a) 'Mission Statement'. Partners HealthCare Systems. Available at *http://www.partners.org/cird/AboutUs.asp?cBox=Miss*. Accessed on February 18, 2008.

Clinical Informatics Research & Development (2008b) ‘Partners HealthCare CIRD Current Projects’. Partners HealthCare Systems. Available at *http://www.partners.org/cird/StaffPrj.asp?cBox=CurrProj*. Accessed on February 18, 2008.

Connolly, Dan (2003) ‘XML Development History’. Available at *http://www.w3.org/XML/hist2002*. Accessed on October 8, 2007.

Davies, Kevin (2006) ‘Search and Deploy’. *Bio-IT World*, October 16: 24–33. Available at *http://www.bio-itworld.com/issues/2006/oct/biogen-idec*. Accessed on March 8, 2008.

de Bruijn, Jos (2004) ‘Ontology Mediation’. SeKT. Available at *http://www.keapro.net/sekt/m_ontology_mediation.htm*. Accessed on February 18, 2008.

Denny, Michael (2002) ‘Ontology Building: A Survey of Editing Tools’. XML.com. Available at *http://www.xml.com/pub/a/2002/11/06/ontologies.html*. Accessed on February 18, 2008.

Denny, Michael (2004) ‘Ontology Tools Survey, Revisited’. XML.com. Available at *http://www.xml.com/pub/a/2004/07/14/onto.html*. Accessed on February 18, 2008.

DiMasi, J. A., R. W. Hansen, and H. G. Grabowski (2003) ‘The Price of Innovation: New Estimates of Drug Development Costs’. *Journal of Health Economics*, 22.2: 151–85. Available at *http://www.panopharma.com/dimasi2003.pdf*. Accessed on March 18, 2008.

Dorsey, M. J., et al. (2006) ‘Assessment of Adrenal Suppression in Children with Asthma Treated with Inhaled Corticosteroids: Use of Dehydroepiandrosterone Sulfate as a Screening Test’. *Annals of Allergy, Asthma & Immunology*, 97.2: 182–6.

Dublin Core Metadata Initiative (2007) ‘About the Initiative’. OCLC. Available at *http://dublincore.org/about/*. Accessed on February 18, 2008.

El-Hoshy, Lynn M. (1998) 'Charting a Changing Language with LCSH'. Library of Congress. Available at *http://www.loc.gov/loc/lcib/9808/lcsh-lan.html*. Accessed on February 18, 2008.

Entertainment Software Association (2008) 'Computer and Video Game Industry Reaches $18.85 Billion in 2007'. Available at *http://www.theesa.com/archives/2008/01/computer_and_vi_1.php*. Accessed on February 17, 2008.

Fallows, Deborah (2005) *Search Engine Users*. Washington DC: Pew Internet & American Life Project. Available at *http://www.pewinternet.org/pdfs/PIP_Searchengine_users.pdf*. Accessed on March 8, 2008.

Feigenbaum, Lee, et al. (2007) 'The Semantic Web in Action'. *Scientific American Magazine*, 297.6: 90–7.

Finn, Peter (2002) 'Hamburg's Cauldron of Terror'. *Washington Post*, September 11. Available at *http://www.washingtonpost.com/wp-dyn/articles/A64793-2002Sep10_4.html*. Accessed on February 18, 2008.

Francis, W. N., and H. Kucera (1979) 'Brown Corpus Manual'. Brown University. Available at *http://khnt.hit.uib.no/icame/manuals/brown/INDEX.HTM*. Accessed on February 15, 2008.

Gaynor, Edward (1996) 'From MARC to Markup: SGML and Online Library Systems'. University of Virginia Library. Available at *http://xml.coverpages.org/gaynorMARC96.html*. Accessed on February 18, 2008.

Gene Ontology Consortium (2008) 'Ontology Downloads'. Gene Ontology Consortium. Available at *http://www.geneontology.org/GO.downloads.ontology.shtml*. Accessed on February 18, 2008.

Gilmore, Jim (2002) 'Frontline: The Man Who Knew'. Public Broadcasting Service. Available at *http://www.pbs.org/wgbh/pages/frontline/shows/knew/could/*. Accessed on February 18, 2008.

Goldfarb, Charles F. (1997) 'SGML: The Reason Why and the First Published Hint', *Journal of the American Society for Information Science*, 48.7: 656–61. Available at *http://www.sgmlsource.com/history/jasis.htm*. Accessed on March 8, 2008.

Gruber, T. R. (1993) 'A Translation Approach to Portable Ontologies'. *Knowledge Acquisition*, 5.2: 199–220. Available at *http://ksl-web.stanford.edu/KSL_Abstracts/KSL-92-71.html*. Accessed on March 8, 2008.

Gruber, Tom (2008) 'Ontology'. In *Encyclopedia of Database Systems*, eds. Ling Liu and M. Tamer Özsu. New York: Springer-Verlag.

Hepp, Martin (2007) 'Possible Ontologies: How Reality Constrains the Development of Relevant Ontologies'. IEEE Computer Society. Available at *http://www.heppnetz.de/files/IEEE-IC-PossibleOntologies-published.pdf*. Accessed on February 18, 2008.

Herman, Ivan, Ralph Swick, and Dan Brickley (2007) 'Resource Description Framework (RDF)'. World Wide Web Consortium. Available at *http://www.w3.org/RDF/*. Accessed on October 8, 2007.

Hill, Eleanor (2002) 'The Intelligence Community's Knowledge of the September 11 Hijackers Prior to September 11, 2001'. Federation of American Scientists. Available at *http://www.fas.org/irp/congress/2002_hr/092002hill.html*. Accessed on February 18, 2008.

Hodges, Andrew (2007) 'Alan Turing: A Short Biography'. Available at *http://www.turing.org.uk/bio/part5.html*. Accessed on April 14, 2007.

Hongsermeier, Tonya (2006) 'From the Bench All the Way to Bedside Clinical Decision Support: The Role of Semantic Technologies in a Knowledge Management Infrastructure for Translational Medicine'. World Wide Web Consortium. Available at *http://www.w3.org/2001/*

sw/hcls/f2f-2006/presentations/Semantic%20Web%20Bench%20to%20Bedside.ppt. Accessed on February 17, 2008.

Hongsermeier, Tonya, Vipul Kashyap, and Margarita Sordo (2007) 'Knowledge Management Infrastructure: Evolution at Partners HealthCare System'. In *Clinical Decision Support: The Road Ahead*, ed. Robert A. Greenes. Boston, MA: Elsevier Academic Press, 447–68.

International Organization for Standardization (1999) 'ISO/IEC 13250: Topic Maps'. ISO. Available at *http://www1.y12.doe.gov/capabilities/sgml/sc34/document/0129.pdf*. Accessed on April 4, 2008.

Johansson, Stig, Geoffrey N. Leech, and Helen Goodluck (1978) *Manual of Information to Accompany the Lancaster-Oslo/Bergen Corpus of British English, For Use With Digital Computers*. Oslo: University of Oslo, Department of English.

Kalyanpur, Aditya, Bijan Parsia, and James Hendler (2005) 'A Tool for Working with Web Ontologies'. *International Journal on Semantic Web and Information Systems*, 1.1: 36–49. Available at *http://www.mindswap.org/papers/Swoop-Journal.pdf*. Accessed on March 8, 2008.

Kashyap, Vipul, Alfredo Morales, and Tonya Hongsermeier (2005) 'Creation and Maintenance of Implementable Clinical Guideline Specifications'. World Wide Web Consortium. Available at *http://www.w3.org/2005/04/swls/clinical_guidelines.pdf*. Accessed on February 17, 2008.

Kashyap, Vipul, et al. (2005) 'Definitions Management: A Semantics-based Approach for Clinical Documentation in Healthcare Delivery'. *Lecture Notes in Computer Science*, 3729: 887–901. Available at *http://www.w3.org/2005/04/ swls/iswc_final_submission.pdf*. Accessed on March 8, 2008.

King, Brandy E. (2006) 'Boolean vs. Semantic Search Interfaces: Which Work Better?' Paper presented at the Special Libraries Association Annual Conference, Baltimore, MD. SLA Contributed Papers. Available at *http://www.sla.org/PDFs/2006CPKing.pdf*. Accessed on March 8, 2008.

Library of Congress (2007) 'MARC Standards'. Library of Congress. Available at *http://www.loc.gov/marc/*. Accessed on February 18, 2008.

Mannes, Aaron, and Jennifer Golbeck (2005) 'Building a Terrorism Ontology'. MINDSWAP. Available at *http://mindswap.org/papers/TerrorOntologyfinal.pdf*. Accessed on June 16, 2007.

Mannes, Aaron, and Jennifer Golbeck (2007) 'Ontology Building: A Terrorism Specialist's Perspective', *Proceedings of the IEEE Aerospace Conference*, Big Sky, MT: IEEE, 1–5.

Manola, Frank, and Eric Miller (2004) 'RDF Primer'. World Wide Web Consortium. Available at *http://www.w3.org/TR/rdf-primer/*. Accessed on February 18, 2008.

Meuller III, Robert S. (2002) 'Statement for the Record – Joint Intelligence Committee Inquiry'. Federation of American Scientists. Available at *http://www.fas.org/irp/congress/2002_hr/092602mueller.html*. Accessed on February 18, 2008.

Morato, Jorge, et al. (2004) 'WordNet Applications'. *The Second Global Wordnet Conference*, Brno, Czech Republic: Global Wordnet Association.

Moutoux, Eugene R. (2008) 'Sentence Diagrams: One Way of Learning English Grammar'. Gene Moutoux. Available at *http://www.geocities.com/gene_moutoux/gettysburg1.htm*. Accessed on February 18, 2008.

Nelson, T. H. (1978) *Dream Machines: New Freedoms Through Computer Screens – A Minority Report*. South Bend, IN: The Distributors.

Newmeyer, Frederick J. (2008) 'The History of Linguistics'. Linguistic Society of America. Available at *http://www.lsadc.org/info/ling-fields-history.cfm*. Accessed on February 15, 2008.

Oates, Stephen B. (1994) *With Malice Toward None: A Life of Abraham Lincoln*. New York: HarperPerennial.

OCLC (2007) 'Dewey Services: Dewey Decimal Classification'. Available at *http://www.oclc.org/dewey*. Accessed on April 14, 2007.

Ontotext (2008) 'The KIM Platform: Semantic Annotation'. Ontotext. Available at *http://www.ontotext.com/kim/semanticannotation.html*. Accessed on February 18, 2008.

Postilnik, Anatoly, et al. (2006) 'Smart Form Framework as a Foundation for Clinical Documentation Platform'. *AMIA Annuual Symposium Proceedings*, 1067. Available at *http://www.pubmedcentral.nih.gov/articlerender.fcgi?artid=1839465*. Accessed on March 8, 2008.

Program for Cooperative Cataloging (2008) 'LC Subject Heading Change Guidelines'. Library of Congress. Available at *http://www.loc.gov/catdir/pcc/saco/sacochghelp.html*. Accessed on February 18, 2008.

Protégé (2008) 'About the Protégé Team'. Protégé. Available at *http://protege.stanford.edu/aboutus/aboutus.html*. Accessed on February 18, 2008.

Roberts, Donald F., Ulla G. Foehr, and Victoria J. Rideout (2005) *Generation M: Media in the Lives of 8–18 Year-olds*. Menlo Park, CA: Kaiser Family Foundation. Available at *http://www.kff.org/entmedia/upload/Generation-M-Media-in-the-Lives-of-8-18-Year-olds-Report.pdf*. Accessed on March 8, 2008.

Roberts, P. M., Hayes, W. S. (2008) 'Information Needs and the Role of Text Mining in Drug Development'. Pacific Symposium on Biocomputing 13: 592–603. Available at *http://psb.stanford.edu/psb-online/proceedings/psb08/roberts.pdf*. Accessed on March 18, 2008.

Sampson, Geoffrey (2008) 'The SUSANNE Analytic Scheme: The Need for Grammatical Taxonomy'. Available at *http://www.grsampson.net/RSue.html*. Accessed on February 18, 2008.

Shadbolt, Nigel, Wendy Hall, and Tim Berners-Lee (2006) 'The Semantic Web Revisited'. IEEE Intelligent Systems. Available at *http://eprints.ecs.soton.ac.uk/12614/1/Semantic_Web_Revisted.pdf*. Accessed on March 13, 2007.

TopicMaps.Org Authoring Group (2001) 'XML Topic Maps (XTM) 1.0'. TopicMaps.Org. Available at *http://topicmaps.org/xtm/index.html*. Accessed on February 18, 2008.

Treverton, Gregory F. (2004) 'Balancing Security and Liberty in the War on Terror'. Maxwell School of Syracuse University. Available at *http://www.maxwell.syr.edu/campbell/Past%20Events/Papers/ISHS/Treverton.pdf*. Accessed on February 18, 2008.

Turing, Alan M. (1950) 'Computing Machinery and Intelligence'. *Mind*, 59: 433–60. Available at *http://www.loebner.net/Prizef/TuringArticle.html*. Accessed on March 8, 2008.

United States Census Bureau (2007) 'NAPCS Product List for NAICS 52: Finance and Insurance'. U.S. Census Bureau. Available at *http://www.census.gov/eos/http://www/napcs/papers/52_12_19_06.pdf*. Accessed on October 8, 2007.

University of Pennsylvania (1999) 'The Penn Treebank Project Corpus'. Available at *http://www.cis.upenn.edu/~treebank/*. Accessed on February 15, 2008.

Vandewater, Elizabeth A., et al. (2007) 'Digital Childhood: Electronic Media and Technology Use Among Infants, Toddlers, and Preschoolers'. *Pediatrics*, 119.5: e1006–15.

von Neumann, John (1958) *The Computer and the Brain*. New Haven, CT: Yale University Press.

W3-Corpora Project (1998) 'The Brown Corpus'. University of Essex, Department of Language and Linguistics. Available at *http://www.essex.ac.uk/linguistics/clmt/w3c/corpus_ling/content/corpora/list/private/brown/brown.html*. Accessed on February 18, 2008.

Wiegler, Laurie (2007) 'OHSU Proposes Wiki-Styled Thesaurus for Relationship-Oriented Text Mining'. *BioInform*, May 25.

Wiseman, Geoffrey (2006) 'Real-World Rule Engines'. InfoQ. Available at *http://www.infoq.com/articles/Rule-Engines*. Accessed on February 18, 2008.

WordNet 3.0 (2008) 'Car'. Princeton University. Available at *http://dictionary.reference.com/browse/car*. Accessed on February 18, 2008.

World Wide Web Consortium (2004a) 'OWL Web Ontology Language: Overview'. W3C. Available at *http://www.w3.org/TR/owl-features/*. Accessed on February 18, 2008.

World Wide Web Consortium (2004b) 'OWL Web Ontology Language: Use Cases and Requirements'. W3C. Available at *http://www.w3.org/TR/2004/REC-webont-req-20040210/#onto-def*. Accessed on April 14, 2007.

World Wide Web Consortium (2008) 'XML Schema'. W3C. Available at *http://www.w3.org/XML/Schema*. Accessed on February 18, 2008.

Wright, Adam, et al. (2007) 'A Description and Functional Taxonomy of Rule-based Decision Support Content at a Large Integrated Delivery Network'. *Journal of the American Medical Informatics Association*, 14.4: 489–96.

Yi, Szu-ting (2007) 'Robust Semantic Role Labeling Using Parsing Variations and Semantic Classes'. Dissertation, University of Pennsylvania.

Zaino, Jennifer (2007) 'Semantic Tools Becoming Easier to Develop'. SemanticWeb.com. Available at *http://www.semanticweb.com/article.php/12160_3713496_1*. Accessed on February 18, 2008.

Index

FSC
www.fsc.org
MIX
Papier | Fördert
gute Waldnutzung
FSC® C083411

Kolibri 360 GmbH
Ferdinand-Jühlke-Straße 7
99095 Erfurt, Deutschland
produktsicherheit@kolibri360.de